"If you're curious about the often-overlooked female prophets in the Bible and eager to understand God's voice, Rachael Groll's new book *Knowing God's Voice* is an essential read. Rachael masterfully bridges the gap in prophetic understanding, exploring a topic many believers find underemphasized or overstressed. By highlighting the powerful examples of female prophets, she offers a refreshing perspective on how these extraordinary women recognized and trusted God's voice. This book is a beacon for anyone seeking a balanced approach to understanding prophecy as a spiritual gift firmly rooted in biblical truth."

Latasha Morrison, *New York Times* bestselling author of *Be the Bridge*; CEO and founder of Be the Bridge

Knowing
GOD'S VOICE

KNOWING GOD'S VOICE

WHAT FEMALE PROPHETS OF THE BIBLE TEACH US ABOUT RECOGNIZING, TRUSTING, AND OBEYING GOD

RACHAEL GROLL

a division of Baker Publishing Group
Grand Rapids, Michigan

Published by Revell
a division of Baker Publishing Group
Grand Rapids, Michigan
RevellBooks.com

Printed in Colombia

Library of Congress Cataloging-in-Publication Data
Names: Groll, Rachael, author.
Title: Knowing God's voice : what female prophets of the Bible teach us about recognizing, trusting, and obeying God / Rachael Groll.
Description: Grand Rapids, Michigan : Revell, a division of Baker Publishing Group, [2025]
Identifiers: LCCN 2025000821 | ISBN 9780800746902 (paperback) | ISBN 9781493451456 (ebook)
Subjects: LCSH: Women in the Bible. | Women—Religious aspects—Christianity. | Christian women—Religious life.
Classification: LCC BS575 .G747 2025 | DDC 220.8/3054—dc23/eng/20250215
LC record available at https://lccn.loc.gov/2025000821

The names and details of the people and situations described in this book have been changed or presented in composite form in order to ensure the privacy of those with whom the author has worked.

Cover image, *Courage and Tenderness*, by Aeron and Tracy Brown
Cover design by Chris Kuhatschek

Author is represented by Capital Literary.

Baker Publishing Group publications use paper produced from sustainable forestry practices and postconsumer waste whenever possible.

25 26 27 28 29 30 31 7 6 5 4 3 2 1

To my Oskavon family,
because our greatness is found
in His embrace.

Contents

PART 3 HULDAH

PART 4 ANNA

PART 5 ENCOURAGEMENT FOR TODAY'S PROPHETS

Author Note

Writing a book about the female prophets in Scripture is a project that was birthed in my heart several years ago. After studying Deborah in depth, I knew she was a topic we needed to unpack within the body of Christ. I knew that God was continuing to call me to help others hear His voice more clearly. And finally, He opened the door for me to sit down and write.

However, when it came time to actually start working, I felt . . . something.

Was it intimidation?

Was it insecurity?

What was behind my procrastination?

As I sat with my cup of coffee, I looked around the house. Everything was done. My schedule was cleared. There was nothing left to do before I "got started." As I reflected on the feeling in my heart, my thoughts surfaced as a prayer.

What if . . . I actually have nothing to say?

What if . . . after all the work of getting to this place, after all my research and time invested, I don't have anything to say that hasn't already been said?

And that is when I heard it. That still, small voice, so loud and clear.

What if I do?

Okay. Thanks for the reminder, Lord.

Here we go, then. Let's start talking about what happens *when we hear from God.*

Introduction

Hey, sis! I am so glad you picked up this book. If I am honest, I find myself wondering why you did. I wonder if it's the same reason I wrote it—to learn more about what prophecy means and to learn more about the female prophets in the Bible. It's hard to find information about them. Most books about prophets cover all the guys. But there are some powerful examples of strong female leaders in Scripture who the Lord used in some pretty extraordinary ways.

Prophecy is one of those topics that seems polarizing to many believers today. For some, it's a word that is hardly ever mentioned in their churches. There are very few Bible studies or Wednesday night classes on the prophetic, which leads to a general ignorance of the topic. For others, there seems to be too much emphasis on prophecy. A "prophetic word" is given almost every time the church doors are open, and it is difficult to separate the divine from the emotional. The reality is that there needs to be some middle ground, where prophecy is seen as valuable within the body of Christ. It should be celebrated as a spiritual gift but taught in a way that is true to the Bible.

I remember one of the first times I received a prophetic word from the Lord. I honestly didn't know what to do with it. At the time, it didn't seem to make sense. I had never been in a church that taught about prophecy; pastors seemed to skip right over prophecy whenever they got to those Bible verses. If there was teaching about it, it was always in the past tense, never as a current way that God operates. Quite honestly, people I knew who claimed to have a prophetic gifting scared me a little. Yet I knew in my spirit that what I was hearing was clearly from the Lord.

It was early January, the time of year when I typically fast after an indulgent holiday season. I take that time to specifically pray for the Lord to give me direction, wisdom, and vision for the coming year. Up until that point, I would get the cliché "word for the year" kind of direction. But this year something else was happening. Instead of giving me a word to home in on, study, read about, journal about, and focus on, God gave me a verse from Scripture:

> But seek first His kingdom and His righteousness, and all these things will be provided to you. (Matt. 6:33 NASB)

This was a familiar verse for me, as I am sure it is for many of you. Yet throughout my week of fasting, this verse became so embedded in my spirit that it was undeniable that God was speaking it loud and clear. In my Scripture reading: Seek first the kingdom. In my worship: Seek first the kingdom. In my devotional reading: Seek first the kingdom. As I listened during prayer: Seek first the kingdom. As I spent the week seeking the Lord, fasting for wisdom, and trying to understand,

I sensed that these sacred echoes were calling me to more than just a reminder of these words. I had a feeling that this phrase, this Scripture, was something the Lord would use either in my own life or in the lives of those around me.

This brings me to an important point that I want to make sure we are clear about as we start studying the female prophets of Scripture and the spiritual gift of prophecy: The primary way that God speaks to us is through His Word. If God gives us a prophetic word, it will never contradict what He says in the Scriptures.

The Bible reveals God's character and nature, which do not change. He is the same today as He was when those pages were written so many years ago. He will not contradict Himself.

So the very first litmus test for a prophetic word is making sure it lines up with the Scriptures and how God reveals Himself to us.

I realized that there was something different about how God was using this Scripture in my life. Not knowing what to do with this information or whom to ask, I tucked the verse away in my journal, telling only my husband about it.

At the time, I was involved in an outreach ministry I had started, working with people I loved. We were ministering to children and families in low-income housing areas in our community. I had written my first book after a difficult season in which some local governing authorities had tried to shut us down. We worked with Alliance Defending Freedom to win back the right to minister in the community, spotlighting our ministry. As a result, we went from two sites locally to ten. I was helping other churches start similar programs, developing curriculum and resources for them to use. Simply put, I loved the ministry God had placed me in and truly felt called to the work.

However, I started to sense a restlessness in my spirit. Perhaps it wasn't restlessness; maybe it was preparation. I could feel a transition was coming. I had gone through ministry transitions before, as the Lord moved me from children's pastor to outreach pastor, burdening my heart for local and global missions. But this time was different. I started having dreams about things that didn't make sense. I felt like I was walking around the house in the black of night. I knew my way around but was still bumping into things, trying to figure out where I was going. I entered into a new kind of prayer life as I earnestly sought the Lord for direction. As I continued to ask Him what was happening, I got the same answer.

Seek first the kingdom.

I didn't know what God wanted me to do, but I kept pressing in to that phrase, examining my heart for whatever God was trying to reveal.

About four months later, things started to make sense. I was offered a job working as the director of spiritual care for a global orphan care organization. I didn't see that coming. On the one hand, everything about the role excited me. After I read the job description out loud to my husband, he asked me if I had written it for myself. It seemed as if everything I had done over the years had been preparing me for this role. But on the other hand . . . my kids. Not my actual kids but my outreach kids. The ones I had found in the street, hungry and broken, who were now thriving and loving Jesus. The kids I had advocated for, testified in court cases for, and helped move into safe spaces. The ones who got a hug only if it came from me or got new shoes only when I found partner organizations to sponsor them. The ones I fought with school districts and summer camps over. Those kids. The ones who had stolen my heart and I had spent the better part of a decade serving.

Almost immediately I heard that familiar voice, and tearfully I realized everything was starting to make sense.

Seek first the kingdom.

On a good week, I was able to help maybe two hundred kids in our small town of thirteen thousand people. But in this new role, which God clearly knew was coming, I would have the opportunity to help thousands of children across the globe. Beyond that, the job involved reaching thousands of families with the hope of the gospel. It meant stepping into a new ministry season beyond anything I had ever hoped for or dreamt about.

God knew it was coming. He always does.

He knew this change would feel too big for me. That I would feel too emotionally attached to "my kids" to let them go. He knew where my heart was and how seriously I took the call He had given me to serve locally. He knew I would feel unqualified and insecure. So He had prepared my heart with a prophetic word. For months, that phrase had consumed me.

Seek first the kingdom.

Not knowing what it meant, I had prayed for the strength to be obedient to whatever God wanted. I had asked Him over and over to reveal it to me. I had committed to the surrender it would mean, in whatever capacity He would call me.

While I didn't see this coming, I knew that if I stayed in a place where my impact was a fraction of the size it could be in the new role, it would be an act of disobedience. That may sound odd at first, thinking that staying in a ministry role would be disobedience; for me, it would have been. God had been revealing to me, for months, that a transition was coming and that my deciding factor would be to put the kingdom first. Not the kingdom of Rachael. Not the kingdom of the ministry I was serving in. Not even the kingdom of the new ministry. The kingdom of God. Where would I be able to be used the most to make the most impact for God's kingdom? The answer was clear.

Sometimes a prophetic word is for a people group as they head into a spiritual battle. Sometimes a prophetic word is meant to encourage or build up a body of believers for a specific reason or to heal something that is broken. But sometimes a prophetic word is for an individual—for you, for me. Part of understanding this spiritual gift is learning to trust the voice of the One who loves us the most. God is not just our Father; He is our *good* Father. He loves us and longs to have a close relationship with us. He desires to have the kind of intimacy and communication with us that is revealed in the pages of Scripture.

God does not change. While on the surface many of us would agree with that statement, do we really live that way? Do we live like we believe what the Bible reveals about God? Do we live like we believe that He wants to be actively involved in our lives? Sadly, for so many believers, the answer is no.

So, this book on prophecy will teach us what it means to lean into communicating with God—in the sense of both the spiritual gift of prophecy and understanding how to hear God's voice more clearly in our own lives. It will do this by looking carefully at the female prophets in Scripture and how God worked in their lives.

Why the women?

Well, for starters, do you know their stories? Could you name the female prophets in the Old Testament? Or in the New? In full transparency, before I started the research for this book, I couldn't. That's embarrassing to admit, but if I have been through seminary (twice!) and have spent so much time in ministry without being able to recall their names (let alone their stories), I think it's safe to assume many women may be in the same place.

There is also something I have learned over the years. It doesn't matter if I am in the bush somewhere in Africa, on the subway in Brooklyn, or in a small group at the local church in my small town: Women seem to have the same insecurities. We have a tendency to doubt when God is speaking to us. Even if we are blessed to be in a church that teaches about spiritual gifts in a healthy, biblical way, we still tend to miss God's voice. We think prophetic words are only for the men. Or we second-guess ourselves, thinking what we hear is just our own emotions. We doubt that God is really speaking to us, and we long to learn how to hear His voice more clearly.

So, sis, my prayer is that this book would not only be an invitation to learn about the prophetesses in Scripture but also about your own relationship with the Lord. I pray that you will walk away from this book with tools to help you grow and encourage other women in your life. I pray that this book will amplify God's voice so that you can be confident in what He is calling you to do. And I pray that you will be empowered and equipped to be a woman who can boldly say that you know Him and want to make Him known.

As I said before, I didn't know the stories of the women I am about to share before I studied them. In theory, I did. I recognized the women's names. I knew these women were important examples. But I didn't *know* them. I had rarely heard their names mentioned, and when I had, it was usually within the context of their being an exception. Friends, these women are not an exception. They reveal God's heart to use both men *and* women to accomplish His plans and purposes. So, as we move forward, here is what you can expect:

For each woman, we will take a look at her role within Scripture. I will explain some things about the history, the culture, and perhaps the time period in which her story unfolded. I will unpack the things that are relevant to us. One of the things that I love about Scripture is that it reveals to us God's character and nature, which does not change. We can learn so much about God from the stories of these women, and those lessons can have an impact on our own lives today. I will also include some personal testimonies of how God has worked in my own life. While the lessons we can learn from studying these women are powerful, my hope is that these testimonies will help you see how God might want to work in your own life. Because, friend, He wants to work in your life. He wants to use you to impact the world around you. Of that, I am confident.

What you will often find as we move through these pages together is that I repeat passages of Scripture. I do that intentionally. I think so often we race through a passage, we check off a little box that says we read our verses for the day, and then an hour later we forget what we read. At least, that's what happens to me. Or sometimes we may remember what we read, but it's hard to understand what it means for us today. So I encourage reading the same passage until you understand it. From a comprehension standpoint, this is helpful because we have trained our brains to have short attention spans. From a spiritual perspective, we have to remember these are *God's* words. He *wants* to speak to us through them. Meditating on God's Word helps us understand what He wants to say to us. Remember, God's Word is the primary way He speaks to us today. We learn to recognize His voice by reading His Word.

As we dive in together, I encourage you to spend some time in prayer to prepare your heart. Perhaps put on some worship music or journal your thoughts. Maybe gather a handful of Scripture passages that you can meditate on as we start this journey together. I can tell you what I am going to do first as I prepare to engage with all of you through these chapters:

Seek first the kingdom.

You've got this, sis. Let's dive in.

♡ Rach

QUESTIONS TO PONDER

- Are there any fears or insecurities you may have to wrestle with on this topic? Even if you don't want to admit them out loud to anyone else, God already knows what they are. Don't be afraid to be honest with Him.
- What does it mean for you to "seek first the kingdom"? Are you currently doing that? How might your life look different if you actively practiced that principle?
- How might your experience be different if you invited the Lord into that conversation in your mind? He longs to not just hear you pray but actually answer you. Allow space and time for Him to respond.
- Does the Lord's voice sound loud and clear to you, even if it is still and small? If so, what might the Lord be telling you as you start this book?
- If you are in a season of finding it difficult to hear His voice, why do you think that is? Are there any barriers getting in the way between you and God? Pray about what those might be and surrender them to the only One who can take them away.

Spend some time in prayer about the things that are coming up for you as you think about the content we are going to study together. Ask God to reveal anything He wants you to pay attention to as we study together.

PART 1

MIRIAM

ONE

The Legacy of a Mother

As we open up our study about the prophetic women of Scripture, we are going to start at the beginning. Very early on, we learn about a woman who is the first to be called a prophetess in Scripture: Miriam. However, Miriam's story actually begins long before we ever learn her name. It starts with her mother, Jochebed. Do you remember her? If not, it's okay. That's why I thought I would include her story.

> Now a man of the tribe of Levi married a Levite woman, and she [Jochebed] became pregnant and gave birth to a son. When she saw that he was a fine child, she hid him for three months. But when she could hide him no longer, she got a papyrus basket for him and coated it with tar and pitch. Then she placed the child in it and put it among the reeds along the bank of the Nile. His sister [Miriam] stood at a distance to see what would happen to him.
>
> Then Pharaoh's daughter went down to the Nile to bathe, and her attendants were walking along the riverbank. She

> saw the basket among the reeds and sent her female slave to get it. She opened it and saw the baby. He was crying, and she felt sorry for him. "This is one of the Hebrew babies," she said.
>
> Then his sister asked Pharaoh's daughter, "Shall I go and get one of the Hebrew women to nurse the baby for you?"
>
> "Yes, go," she answered. So the girl went and got the baby's mother. Pharaoh's daughter said to her, "Take this baby and nurse him for me, and I will pay you." So the woman took the baby and nursed him. When the child grew older, she took him to Pharaoh's daughter and he became her son. She named him Moses, saying, "I drew him out of the water." (Exod. 2:1–10)

The story of Miriam starts long before we see her appear on the edge of the Nile as a young girl. Miriam's story starts with a legacy of faith handed down through her family. Likely before she could understand the words being said, Miriam heard the prayers of her parents as they sought the wisdom of the Lord. Both of her parents were from the tribe of Levi, the priestly line of the Hebrew people. It was this tribe that God set apart to stand in the gap between Yahweh and the Israelites. The lineage that led to the family that included siblings Moses, Miriam, and Aaron had served the Lord faithfully for generations. Perhaps those who have been born into a family of faith can understand what it must have been like to live within a culture of faith since birth.

At this time in Israel's history, when it was very difficult to be a follower of God, as the oppression of the Hebrew people in Egypt was intense, Moses was born to Jochebed and Amram. Despite the command of Pharaoh that all baby boys be thrown into the Nile, Jochebed hid Moses, knowing that doing so could have severe consequences. It was only a matter of time before the sleepy newborn would grow old enough to be found, yet we see Jochebed act with wisdom that surely was from the Lord.

When I think back over how I learned this story in Sunday school, I remember questioning why little baby Moses didn't just sink into the river in his boat made of leaves. Now I realize it was because of the wisdom and strategy the Lord gave his mother.

Jochebed started by crafting a small boat out of papyrus reeds for baby Moses. To this day, Egyptians know something about reeds that you and I may not. Crocodiles are scared of them. They tend to stay away from the reeds, and often boats are made of three layers of reeds or have bunches of reeds attached to them. While not foolproof, it's a way to keep the crocodile-infested waters a little safer.

To waterproof the tiny boat, Jochebed used bitumen, which was a slime made out of the mud from the bottom of the Nile. When it dried, the bitumen formed a waterproof seal, also known as pitch. Do you remember hearing about pitch anywhere else in Scripture? Noah used pitch to seal the ark. The basket that Jochebed made was a pitch-covered, crocodile-repelling mini boat that had the same waterproofing as the ark, which had stayed afloat during forty days of rain!

The wisdom of Jochebed didn't stop with the construction of Moses's boat. She also had a strategy behind where she placed this little boat. Scripture says she placed the boat among the reeds along the edge of the water. Contrary to what we see in our Sunday school coloring pages, she didn't place the basket *in* the water. She placed it *next* to the water. It would have only *looked* like the boat had drifted there. The location she chose was where the royals regularly went to wash, which was likely blocked off from the rest of the river . . . and most of the crocodiles. How did Jochebed know where to place baby Moses in his basket? She was a watcher. She watched the princess's routine to see where and when she went there.

After watching, planning, and strategizing, Miriam's mother showed extraordinary courage and faith to release the basket. Jochebed needed to trust God for His part in the plan. She worked hard, with wisdom and strategy on her part. But at a certain point, she had to let go and trust God. I think if we had the opportunity to go back and talk to Jochebed, she would tell us that she placed baby Moses not so much in the water as into God's hands.

That's what surrender means. Doing our part, then releasing things into God's hands.

Often, that is how God works in our lives. He gives us strategy, wisdom, and a plan that takes work on our part. But at a certain point, we have to lay down the very thing that we are clinging to.

Our child.

Our career.

Our dream.

Our pain.

Interestingly enough, the word that is used to describe the reeds in this story is the same word that is used to describe the Red Sea. A better translation in English would actually be the "Reed" Sea. Think through that with me for a moment.

As a baby, Moses was saved from the reeds and the water. Eventually, adult Moses would also be saved from the reeds and the water of the Reed Sea. Miriam was there for both.

There tends to be a persistent experience of God in our lives. A way that He interacts with us and intervenes on our behalf. The beauty of that is it may be different for you than it is for me.

How is God showing up in your life? How has He in the past? Have you ever thought about that connection?

Friend, I want to make something really clear. Whatever it is that God asks you to lay down, you can trust Him with it. I am certain of it.

And this is where Miriam enters the story.

TWO

Shadows of Faith

Now a man of the tribe of Levi married a Levite woman, and she became pregnant and gave birth to a son. When she saw that he was a fine child, she hid him for three months. But when she could hide him no longer, she got a papyrus basket for him and coated it with tar and pitch. Then she placed the child in it and put it among the reeds along the bank of the Nile. His sister [Miriam] stood at a distance to see what would happen to him.

Then Pharaoh's daughter went down to the Nile to bathe, and her attendants were walking along the riverbank. She saw the basket among the reeds and sent her female slave to get it. She opened it and saw the baby. He was crying, and she felt sorry for him. "This is one of the Hebrew babies," she said.

Then his sister asked Pharaoh's daughter, "Shall I go and get one of the Hebrew women to nurse the baby for you?"

"Yes, go," she answered. So the girl went and got the baby's mother. Pharaoh's daughter said to her, "Take this baby and nurse him for me, and I will pay you." So the woman took the baby and nursed him. When the child grew older, she

> took him to Pharaoh's daughter and he became her son. She named him Moses, saying, "I drew him out of the water." (Exod. 2:1–10)

Miriam was born a slave. We also have to remember that women and girls did not typically have voices within the culture at that time. Speaking to the daughter of Pharaoh as a young Hebrew slave girl shows a measure of boldness that would become characteristic of Miriam's entire life. We see shadows of the faith Jochebed instilled in her daughter. Jochebed likely taught her to watch, to listen, and, more importantly, that Yahweh was real.

Long before she was called a prophet, Miriam used her voice to speak up, even if there would be a cost. In this case, because of her boldness, her baby brother had more time with his family, and her family was helped financially for the next couple years.

There was so much wisdom in this young girl, even in how she spoke. Notice the way she phrased the question: "Shall I go and get one of the Hebrew women to nurse the baby for you?" (Exod. 2:7). Miriam asked the question as if the princess had already decided to keep the baby. Perhaps she had. Or perhaps Miriam's words guided the thoughts of the princess toward rescuing the child. Miriam and the princess both knew that allowing the child to live would be in violation of the orders of Pharaoh. Yet Miriam still asked. She still took a risk, asking the question, hoping to influence the answer. Her question appealed to the emotions of the princess, and she leaned into the opportunity on behalf of her little brother.

A crying baby.

A baby who was vulnerable, needing to be fed by his mama.

A baby who, without intervention, would soon die.

A prophetic voice within the body of Christ often does the same thing. It connects the things that break God's heart with those who can do something about them:

vulnerable children
widows
orphans
poverty

A prophet helps make a connection between those who are insulated from the pain of the world and those who are still broken. A prophet stands in the gap so that those with the means can reach in to help those with the lack. A prophet reminds the people of God of the priorities of God.

A prophet helps make a connection between those who are insulated from the pain of the world and those who are still broken.

Privilege, power, and provision are then matched with pain, poverty, and problems. The outcome is often deliverance.

Sometimes I think we forget that prophecy is a gift that God gives the body of Christ—the entire body of Christ. We do not have to be called a "prophet" to have a "prophetic voice." God's voice is the "prophetic voice." Our job is just to say out loud what He shows us or tells us. And most of what He says He has already said in His Word.

If we look at prophecy in Scripture, we can recognize the following:

Less than 2 percent of Old Testament prophecies speak about the Messiah.

Less than 5 percent of Old Testament prophecies speak about the New Testament.

Less than 1 percent of Old Testament prophecies predict events that are to come.[1]

That's a total of only 8 percent of Old Testament prophecies predicting something. The other 92 percent? They speak about what God has already said. They remind God's people of God's words. They call out the things that hurt God's heart and point toward the way He has called us to act as His children.

One of the things we have to remember is that God does not change. He reveals His character and nature to us through the pages of the Scriptures, helping us to understand how He operates today. While there is some nuance, and we now have the help of the Holy Spirit, there are aspects of God's heart for His people that we can clearly see from Scripture. A prophet acts as a sort of bullhorn for God, reminding people of what He has already said.

It can sometimes be challenging to live as a Christian in today's culture. Things seem backward and often don't make sense. But we have a God who says yes when the world says no. I've seen this in my own life, and we see it in the pages of the Bible.

Pharaoh was trying to control the fertility of the Hebrew people by throwing the Hebrew baby boys into the river that he and the Egyptians worshiped. Why did they worship the Nile River? Because they thought it was a source of fertility. Ironic, isn't it? What did God do? That very river was the place Moses was pulled from, and he would be the one to eventually deliver the Hebrew people from the hands of Pharaoh. A baby that Pharaoh was trying to kill ended up being raised in his own palace, where he received the best education, the best nutrition, and the best military training.

Only God.

Have hope, friend, that God is in control, even when it doesn't look like it.

THREE

Song of Miriam

When Pharaoh's horses, chariots and horsemen went into the sea, the Lord brought the waters of the sea back over them, but the Israelites walked through the sea on dry ground. Then Miriam the prophet, Aaron's sister, took a timbrel in her hand, and all the women followed her, with timbrels and dancing. Miriam sang to them:

> "Sing to the Lord,
> for he is highly exalted.
> Both horse and driver
> he has hurled into the sea." (Exod. 15:19–21)

Three verses. This part of Miriam's life is revealed in only three verses, yet within these three verses we learn so much about her.

At this point, Miriam is in her eighties, and she lived most of her life separated from the little brother she helped save so many years ago at the River Nile. In case the details are foggy, here is a brief recap leading up to these verses.

While Moses grew up under the care of Pharaoh, he eventually escaped to the desert after killing an Egyptian who was abusing an Israelite. He became a shepherd and spent forty years away from his family. Then God appeared to Moses in a burning bush, instructing him to help the Israelites escape bondage. Moses returned to Egypt and was reunited with his siblings, Miriam and Aaron. Together, Moses and Aaron went to Pharaoh and told him what the Lord had said: “Let my people go.” This didn’t sit too well with Pharaoh, so he doubled the workload of the Israelite slaves. The Israelite people were, of course, upset by this, but Moses and Aaron refused to give up and returned to Pharaoh again and again, asking him to release God’s people. Pharaoh’s refusal was met each time with a more severe consequence: The Nile turned to blood, frogs covered every surface, all the dust turned to gnats, swarms of flies came, the livestock died, and boils covered the skin of the people and their livestock. Yet Pharaoh’s heart was still hardened against the Lord. After hail, locusts, and darkness failed to get Pharaoh to budge, the final plague came: All the firstborn sons in Egypt were killed; only the children of the Israelites were spared. Pharaoh finally told Moses to take the Israelites and go. Quickly, the Hebrew people packed up and left Egypt, heading into the wilderness.

Before long, Pharaoh regretted his decision and went after the Israelites. They were trapped, with the Red Sea in front of them and Pharaoh behind them. As Pharaoh and his men narrowed in on them, God performed one of the greatest miracles in the Old Testament. He sent a mighty wind that parted the water, and with walls of water on either side of them, the Israelites walked through the sea on dry ground! But when Pharaoh's army started walking the same path, the walls of water collapsed, ending their lives. Moses responded by singing a song of praise to the Lord.

This is the point where our Scripture passage comes in. After Moses finished singing, Miriam picked up where he left off.

> When Pharaoh's horses, chariots and horsemen went into the sea, the LORD brought the waters of the sea back over them, but the Israelites walked through the sea on dry ground. Then Miriam the prophet, Aaron's sister, took a timbrel in her hand, and all the women followed her, with timbrels and dancing. Miriam sang to them:
>
> "Sing to the LORD,
> for he is highly exalted.
> Both horse and driver
> he has hurled into the sea." (Exod. 15:19–21)

One of the first things that strikes me about this passage is that Miriam and the women of Israel took their instruments with them when they left Egypt. They didn't know what was going to happen; they didn't even know where they were going. But they trusted the God who was leading them. When it was time to quickly gather their things and leave Egypt, the women took their instruments for worship. They went forth with an expectation that God was going to show up for them, even though they didn't know what that would look like. They had just seen God deliver them through the miraculous events of the plagues, protecting them each step of the way. They knew that God had delivered them once, and they had the confidence that He would do it again.

Miriam was prepared to praise.

Before she knew the outcome.

Before she saw the miracle.

Before the season in the wilderness was over.

I often wonder what this looks like in my own life. Am I prepared to praise God even when I don't know the outcome? Being prepared to praise before we see the results of God's answers to our prayers is a powerful thing. It reveals how much we trust God—trust Him to show up in our lives, trust Him to answer our prayers, trust Him to do what only He can do. So often we are quick to complain when we are in the seasons of wilderness in our lives.

What would it look like if we instead had a posture of praise even before we saw the dry ground of our miracle? In Miriam's case, and for all the Israelites, there had never been dry ground there before. There hasn't been since. That fact is such an encouragement to me because many times when we are in our seasons of wilderness—waiting for a miracle—we have no idea how things are going to work out. And often God works in ways that don't make sense to us. He works in ways He never has before, at least in our lives.

Sometimes I hesitate when the "dry ground" appears. When God makes a way where there seems to be no way, it can be hard to believe that it actually *is* dry ground, that we actually *can* take that first step.

God has taught me one thing over and over in my life: Delayed obedience is disobedience. God's favor will last only as long as we have the faith to take advantage of it. The Israelites' dry ground was dry for only so long. They had to have the faith to take the first step.

What do you think would have happened if the Israelites had been too fearful to take that first step? The waters weren't parted forever. If they had waited too long, it's very likely they would have died at the hands of Pharaoh. Delayed obedience to God can cost us the blessing of God in our lives, but it can also have lasting consequences, for us and for those around us. We have to reach a place where we don't delay in our obedience, and this happens when we learn to trust God. Trusting God comes from hearing His voice. Learning to hear His voice comes from reading His Word.

Delayed obedience is disobedience.

While scholars continue to debate whether this portion of Scripture should be considered prophetic activity, it is clear that Miriam is called a prophetess. This leads to the second thing I notice in this passage: There seems to be a connection between the gift of prophecy and a heart of worship. Both Miriam and Deborah, whom we will study in the next part, were called prophetesses and are also recorded as authoring songs of victory.

Miriam wasn't just *prepared* to praise. She actually *did* praise. It's not enough just to be prepared; we have to follow through. If we are in a posture of surrender to God, allowing Him to work in our lives, there should be an overflow of praise from our hearts when we see Him move. When we get to the other side of our miracle, our response needs to be praise. There may be elements of our own hard work, intelligence, or finances that play into the resolution of our situation, but we have to realize that without God's help none of those things would matter. Praise for His goodness should always follow the moments when He works in our lives.

In my own life, there has always been a connection between the gift of prophecy and worship. It seems as if worship becomes the avenue that God uses to make my heart ready to hear from Him. Several times I have tried to explain this to others who don't share the same kind of spiritual gift. I have been told that I am wrong or that the prophetic gifting is simply my emotions. Others say that God operates outside of worship when He wants to deliver a prophetic message. While I don't doubt that is true, I think in some cases God connects the two. He does with Miriam and Deborah.

Worship and prophecy are connected in the Old Testament in several other places as well. For example, in 1 Samuel 10, we see this connection when Samuel is instructing Saul:

> "After that you will go to Gibeah of God, where there is a Philistine outpost. As you approach the town, you will meet a procession of prophets coming down from the high place with lyres, timbrels, pipes and harps being played before them, and they will be prophesying. The Spirit of the LORD will come powerfully upon you, and you will prophesy with them; and you will be changed into a different person. Once these signs are fulfilled, do whatever your hand finds to do, for God is with you.
>
> "Go down ahead of me to Gilgal. I will surely come down to you to sacrifice burnt offerings and fellowship offerings, but you must wait seven days until I come to you and tell you what you are to do."

> As Saul turned to leave Samuel, God changed Saul's heart, and all these signs were fulfilled that day. When he and his servant arrived at Gibeah, a procession of prophets met him; the Spirit of God came powerfully upon him, and he joined in their prophesying. When all those who had formerly known him saw him prophesying with the prophets, they asked each other, "What is this that has happened to the son of Kish? Is Saul also among the prophets?" (vv. 5–11)

We also see a connection between worship and prophecy in the life of the prophet Elisha:

> Elisha said, "As surely as the LORD Almighty lives, whom I serve, if I did not have respect for the presence of Jehoshaphat king of Judah, I would not pay any attention to you. But now bring me a harpist."
>
> While the harpist was playing, the hand of the LORD came on Elisha and he said, "This is what the LORD says: I will fill this valley with pools of water. For this is what the LORD says: You will see neither wind nor rain, yet this valley will be filled with water, and you, your cattle and your other animals will drink. This is an easy thing in the eyes of the LORD; he will also deliver Moab into your hands. You will overthrow every fortified city and every major town. You will cut down every good tree, stop up all the springs, and ruin every good field with stones."
>
> The next morning, about the time for offering the sacrifice, there it was—water flowing from the direction of Edom! And the land was filled with water. (2 Kings 3:14–20)

Seeing how God connects worship and prophecy throughout the Scriptures helps us to understand that a heart of worship can be a conduit for hearing from God. For me personally, it is a validation of the experience of a gift that I've received often in my life. It is also so encouraging to see that God does not discriminate in His gift giving. Both men and women have experienced this phenomenon and been called to speak on God's behalf. Miriam had a prophetic gift and was one of the first musicians in Israel's history.

When God validates your gift, the validation of others becomes a little less critical.

Exodus 15:21 eventually became known as the "Song of Miriam" to the Hebrew people. They used this song corporately in worship as they rehearsed God's goodness in their lives. Even in moments when things didn't make sense. When they were still in their wilderness season. When there was more wandering than wondering. When their children started to doubt.

Praise for God's goodness in our lives isn't just for worship leaders or for Sunday mornings. It's how we prepare for God's next move in our lives—by remembering who He was because that is who He will continue to be. We need to remember that the miracles in our lives sometimes weren't visible until they were completed. We can rehearse the victory in our hearts and minds before we see it with our eyes.

Have there been moments when you experienced God's presence or provision? If so, you can use those moments to reveal His goodness to others.

The last thing I recognize from these three short verses is that Miriam had a position of leadership within the nation of Israel. Alongside her brothers, Moses and Aaron, Miriam helped lead God's people. Over two million people. We see this here as she leads a victory song of praise, but it is also mentioned by Yahweh Himself:

I brought you up out of Egypt
and redeemed you from the land of slavery.
I sent Moses to lead you,
also Aaron and Miriam. (Mic. 6:4)

The title "prophetess" reveals that Miriam had a role in speaking to and shepherding the people of Israel as they made their way through the wilderness. As she received messages from the Lord, it was her responsibility to proclaim His word to His people.

His word to His people.

Hearing from God is about God revealing His heart to us, a heart that loves His people. He loved them then, and He loves them now.

Hearing from God will almost always place you in a position of leadership, even if that doesn't mean ministry. It may mean you have influence over the people in your life as you call out the will and purpose of God in certain situations. And when God moves? Praise for His presence should be your response.

FOUR

Leprosy of the Heart

Miriam and Aaron began to talk against Moses because of his Cushite wife, for he had married a Cushite. "Has the LORD spoken only through Moses?" they asked. "Hasn't he also spoken through us?" And the LORD heard this.

(Now Moses was a very humble man, more humble than anyone else on the face of the earth.)

At once the LORD said to Moses, Aaron and Miriam, "Come out to the tent of meeting, all three of you." So the three of them went out. Then the LORD came down in a pillar of cloud; he stood at the entrance to the tent and summoned Aaron and Miriam. When the two of them stepped forward, he said, "Listen to my words:

"When there is a prophet among you,
  I, the LORD, reveal myself to them in visions,
  I speak to them in dreams.
But this is not true of my servant Moses;
  he is faithful in all my house.

> With him I speak face to face,
>   clearly and not in riddles;
>   he sees the form of the LORD.
> Why then were you not afraid
>   to speak against my servant Moses?"

> The anger of the LORD burned against them, and he left them.
>
> When the cloud lifted from above the tent, Miriam's skin was leprous—it became as white as snow. Aaron turned toward her and saw that she had a defiling skin disease, and he said to Moses, "Please, my lord, I ask you not to hold against us the sin we have so foolishly committed. Do not let her be like a stillborn infant coming from its mother's womb with its flesh half eaten away."
>
> So Moses cried out to the LORD, "Please, God, heal her!"
>
> The LORD replied to Moses, "If her father had spit in her face, would she not have been in disgrace for seven days? Confine her outside the camp for seven days; after that she can be brought back." So Miriam was confined outside the camp for seven days, and the people did not move on till she was brought back.
>
> After that, the people left Hazeroth and encamped in the Desert of Paran. (Num. 12:1–16)

The next time we see Miriam after the parting of the Red Sea is about a year later, and she seems almost unrecognizable. The woman who was last seen worshiping and praising God for His hand of faithfulness now takes on almost a completely different personality. Miriam and her brother Aaron come to Moses with a complaint. While there is more bubbling under the surface, their initial complaint is over something that still rears its ugly head within the body of Christ today: prejudice.

What was the big deal about Moses's wife being a Cushite? Who was she?

The only wife of Moses we learn about in Scripture is Zipporah, who was from Midian (Exod. 2:16–22). Some scholars believe the Cushite woman is a second wife Moses took after Zipporah died. Others believe the wife Miriam and Aaron are referring to is actually Zipporah and that Cush and Midian were two names for the same region. The area of Cush is ancient Ethiopia, which means that Moses's wife had much darker skin than the rest of them. It's also possible that his wife was not actually from Cush but looked like she was. The complaint is that Moses is in a mixed-race marriage with a foreigner.

But while the siblings' complaint starts with an attack on their sister-in-law, it really serves as a way to bring up a deeper complaint and to call into question Moses's leadership. Had the Lord been speaking only through Moses? Were they not also used by the Lord to lead the people of Israel?

Let's pause here for a second to point out something. The answer to their second question is yes. God did use Miriam and Aaron. So often people narrow in on patriarchy in the Bible, which was common in the ancient Near East, using it as an excuse to keep women from leadership roles within the body of Christ today. However, we see clearly here that God did include a woman in leadership. He did speak to her, just as He speaks to women today. The issue is not the fact that she is a woman. The issue is her heart.

There is no dispute that both Miriam and Aaron had heard from the Lord within their leadership roles. In fact, the Lord Himself confirms this in Numbers 12:6–8:

> When there is a prophet among you,
>   I, the Lord, reveal myself to them in visions,
>   I speak to them in dreams.
> But this is not true of my servant Moses;
>   he is faithful in all my house.
> With him I speak face to face,
>   clearly and not in riddles;
>   he sees the form of the Lord.

God talks about how He reveals Himself to them in visions and dreams. But He then goes on to talk about the special anointing that is on Moses. Yahweh speaks more clearly to Moses face-to-face. The glory of the Lord rested on Moses so powerfully that after he met with God, his face literally shone for weeks. Moses would go on to author the Torah, the first five books of the Old Testament. There was no denying that the relationship God had with Moses was different from the relationship He had with Miriam and Aaron. Moses is appointed the leader of Israel, and he alone is called the servant of God. Yet while the special anointing on Moses is different, this doesn't mean that Miriam and Aaron don't also have a special anointing.

The gifts that God has given our brother or sister in Christ do not negate the gifts He has given us. We each have a unique blend of experience, personality, temperament, and opportunities. God uses each one of us uniquely. My calling may not be your calling, and that's okay.

The bottom line is that we all share one very important calling, even though it may look different in each of our lives: to know Him and to make Him known.

It is very possible that Miriam and Aaron were responding to the complaints of the people they were leading. We know from the entire exodus story that the people of Israel were complainers. Even when God gave them manna from the sky, water from a rock, and guidance through a cloud by day and fire by night, they still complained. They often longed for the slavery of Egypt in light of the difficulties of the wilderness. Miriam heard the complaints of the people firsthand, perhaps more so than her brothers because of her close proximity to the women. Not that I am saying women are complainers, but . . . if you know, you know.

There likely could have been a better way for Miriam to resolve this issue. It's possible her intentions were good: Moses was a leader and people emulate their leaders. If Moses took a foreign wife, others could follow in his footsteps. It would be dangerous if the Israelites started marrying foreigners because most foreigners did not follow Yahweh as their God. At some point, Aaron agreed with Miriam's thinking, even if she was the one to voice the complaint while he remained silent.

Her mistake, then? Making her complaint in public. By voicing publicly the issue that was festering in her heart, she challenged the authority that God had given Moses in front of the people he was called to lead.

This feels familiar to me. Perhaps it does for you as well. There have been times in my life when I allowed the complaints of others to affect my own thoughts and feelings. Or perhaps they watered the seeds of insecurity that were already in my own heart:

jealousy
bitterness
pride
sarcasm
fear

If I am honest, there have been times in my life when I spoke harsh words that should have been said in private. I am not proud of those moments. Like with Miriam, I think many of them were rooted in good intentions that were overtaken by my own desire to be heard, seen, and acknowledged.

To be right.

To do things *my* way.

The lesson is that we need to be very intentional about guarding our hearts, our minds, *and* our mouths so we don't end up in a place similar to Miriam's.

We see Miriam's heart, full of wisdom, compassion, and worship, move from a posture of praise to one of pride, and there are consequences. By allowing an offense to fester, she ends up attacking the authority that God gave Moses as the leader of the people of Israel. Bad idea.

What happens next? God defends Moses and punishes Miriam. There is some debate as to why Miriam was punished and Aaron wasn't. Perhaps it was because Miriam was the spokesperson for the two. Or perhaps it was because Aaron was the high priest and removing him from the community would have taken away the people's ability to communicate with God and worship. Regardless of the reason, God responds to the way Miriam has disrespected Moses's leadership, authority, and anointing.

In the scene that unfolds next, much is revealed about the difference between Moses's heart and Miriam's.

When Miriam hurls accusations at Moses, he doesn't defend himself. He doesn't have to. God steps in to defend him. Scripture says that Moses is humble, the most humble man on earth. We see this aspect of Moses's character revealed as he pleads to God on Miriam's behalf when he sees the terrible consequences of her words: being struck with leprosy. "Please, God, heal her!" God hears Moses and makes a concession for him, healing her but also removing her from the fellowship of the community for a time of cleansing.

This entire scenario can be hard for us to grasp as modern readers. What is leprosy? Most of us have never seen it in our lifetimes and likely never will, unless we travel to extremely impoverished parts of the world. However, leprosy in the ancient world was quite common and represented several things in that culture.

The Hebrew word *tsaraʿat* ("leprosy") was a general term used to describe any number of skin diseases, including things like eczema and psoriasis. In the Septuagint, it was translated using the Greek word *lepra*, meaning "scaly" or "rough." That's why our English Bibles use the word "leprosy" even though *tsaraʿat* does not necessarily indicate Hansen's disease, the medical condition commonly called leprosy.[1]

Within Israelite culture, *tsaraʿat* was seen as a punishment for things like gossip, slander, and pride. The Old Testament law commanded that those with such skin diseases were to live separately from the rest of the community. Separation served not only to protect the community from physical illness but also to prevent the spread of dangerous attitudes that were rooted in pride.[2]

Do you get the implications here?

Pride infects everything it touches. Slander and gossip will eventually cause us to be removed from the fellowship of God's people, either by the hand of discipline from God or by the natural consequences in our damaged relationships.

Miriam definitely heard from God, yet she allowed her pride to poison her leadership and ended up being completely removed from the people she had been called to serve. It took time for her to be restored to right relationship with her community and her brothers. Because the people of Israel had to wait on her before they could move on, Miriam's pride delayed God's people from following God's plan. There are consequences to our pride.

Now, does this mean that the next time you gossip about your pastor you will be struck with an eczema flare-up? No. (But also, don't gossip about your pastor.) What it does mean is that pride has consequences and that we need to stop it before it infects our entire physical body, our leadership, and our relationships.

In contrast to Miriam's pride, which separated her from the rest of her community, we see Moses's humility. Moses's humility was one of the key factors that enabled God to use him so mightily. His humility allowed God to defend him when he was attacked and to deal with his accusers.

One thing that always strikes me in this passage is that Moses's own siblings were criticizing him. Unfortunately, this is common. When we learn how to hear God's voice, it sometimes doesn't go over so well with our brothers and sisters in Christ. It's not that they can't hear God. But they allow the voices of jealousy and insecurity to speak louder. This is something we all need to guard our hearts, our minds, and our mouths against.

One last note before we move on. Sometimes we overlook the irony in the Bible because we don't always understand the ancient culture to which it was written. For instance, we learn something about *tsara'at* from Aaron:

> Do not let her be like a stillborn infant coming from its mother's womb with its flesh half eaten away. (Num. 12:12)

Aaron is describing a common malady in the ancient world in which babies were born without the pink coloring of most newborns. This form of skin disease made a person's skin completely white. It's a stark contrast to what started this whole thing, an objection to the dark skin of Moses's wife. Did you catch that?

We see you, God. We see you.

FIVE

How to Be Like Miriam

From the moment we see Miriam first appear on the banks of the Nile as a child until the time of her death in the wilderness, we learn about the incredible place she held in Israel's history. There is biblical evidence for the impact Miriam made as a leader, as a worshiper, and as a prophet of God. Let's recap some of the things we learned about Miriam:

She helped rescue her baby brother Moses, who would later be used by God to rescue the Israelites from the hand of Pharaoh (Exod. 2:4).

She served God alongside her brothers, Moses and Aaron, leading the Hebrew people to freedom (Mic. 6:4).

She led the Israelite women in worship and praise after God delivered the Israelites from the Egyptian army, allowing them to cross the Red Sea on dry ground (Exod. 15:19–21).

Miriam served God well into old age, living a life that was dedicated to following Yahweh. Each time we see Miriam in Scripture, it bears witness to her testimony of leadership. But there is something else we need to remember as we learn from this prophetic powerhouse of a woman: Even Miriam got it wrong.

You and I will too.

There will be times when we mess up. Times when we speak out of turn or reveal something that God intended to be private and personal. Times when we forget that there is an important aspect to remember when we read and study the Bible: We always want to make sure we are patterning our lives after the God of the Bible, not the people of the Bible. God is always the hero in the story. We can't try to justify our sin by saying, "It's in the Bible." That's not the way it works. We should always, *always*, pattern our lives—our character—after God.

That being said, there are some powerful lessons we can learn from the life of Miriam, and by reflecting on those lessons, hopefully we can avoid the same pitfalls she encountered.

1. Guard your heart.

We see very clearly that God used Miriam. For many of us, when we start to sincerely seek God and His will for our lives, He will use us within our own circles of influence. When that happens, when God chooses to use us for His glory and we *know* that He has used us, we can be tempted to settle into pride. There is a danger in comparing our experience of God to that of others, which is exactly what we see happen with Miriam. Miriam did play a huge role in how God saved Moses.

I think if I were Miriam, more than once I would have had the thought *If it wasn't for me . . .* Perhaps that feels familiar for you too.

If it wasn't for me . . .

that church wouldn't have gotten that program started.

that person wouldn't have even come to church.

that small group wouldn't have flourished.

that mission trip wouldn't have taken flip-flops.

Insert whatever you helped God do here.

We must be very intentional about guarding our hearts against settling into pride and remembering that it's not about us; it's about God. Instead of thinking *If it wasn't for me . . .* we have to remember instead *If it wasn't for God . . .* When we shift our hearts to that frame of mind, it is so much easier to let the pride go.

Out of all of us, Miriam would seem justified in her pride. Although we don't have a biblical record of her prophecies, Scripture clearly calls her a prophet of Israel. In addition, the Dead Sea Scrolls from the Qumran community record the prophecies of Miriam that were written down by her father, Amram. According to the scrolls, Miriam had a word about Moses that prophesied his leadership of the Israelite people and even some of the details of the parting of the Red Sea.[1] While the Dead Sea Scrolls are not Scripture, they are important documents for the historical record of the Jewish people. Some scholars would argue that the scrolls could have been written in a period when the story of Miriam was already known. Regardless of the timing, the fact that Miriam's prophecies were written down showcases how important she was to the Jewish people. In an age when the testimony of women was not considered valid, the testimony of Miriam was recorded. That is significant and shows us that Miriam made an impact on the people she served.

Often when we are given a place of leadership by God, we are inevitably placed in a position of having a platform. While that may mean different things today than it did during Miriam's time, the result is still the same: Leadership and passion lead to having a platform. Having a platform then leads to two very different outcomes: praise or pride (see fig. 5.1).

Figure 5.1 **Pride and Platform**

Leadership / Passion / Gifting

↓

Platform

↙ ↘

Praise (Outward) | Pride (Inward)

If we allow our leadership to build God's kingdom, then the natural response to the effectiveness of God in our lives will be praise. We will praise God for who He is, for what He has done, and for how He is working in and through us.

If we instead allow our leadership to build a name for ourselves, then we can quickly fall into pride.

The difference? Attention. If we direct our attention outward toward God, we will praise, giving God the glory. But the moment we allow our attention to turn inward, we become prideful. Pride can quickly move like an infection from our hearts to our minds.

That brings us to the second lesson we can learn from Miriam.

2. Guard your mind.

We see Miriam go from a leader who praises God and is confident in her own calling and leadership to a woman who is insecure, comparing herself and her brother Aaron to Moses. The lesson here? Don't compare your calling. The calling of God in your life will be different from the calling of God in someone else's life. Their calling will not negate yours. We are all different parts of the body of Christ, and God equips each of us differently in the way He prepares us to lead within our circles of influence. If we stop comparing our calling and what God has done in our lives to the calling and experiences of others, we can have more joy in how God has uniquely created us to serve Him. I realize that my calling is not your calling, even if you are also called to write and speak and teach about the gospel. Even though our callings may be similar, they are not the same. The people God gives me access to, the places He sends me, and the opportunities He gives me are all different from yours. That does not make either of our callings less valid. That means we can fully lean into what God has called us to do, letting go of any envy about what God has called others to do.

Perhaps you may be thinking at this point, *But I'm not someone who is called.* My response to that? We all are. As believers in the Lord Jesus Christ, we are all called to know Him and to make Him known.

The calling of every Christian is to tell others who Jesus is and what He has done. The way that fleshes out in our individual lives will look different. Sometimes the way that looks for us will look different in different seasons. Comparing our calling or even the way God works at different points in our lives can put up a roadblock for how God wants to use us today.

Guarding our hearts and minds are effective strategies, but they are almost pointless if we aren't also intentional with the next lesson we see in the life of Miriam.

3. Guard your mouth.

Okay. Time for some vulnerability here. This one is always my biggest struggle. It's always my mouth that gets me in trouble. I really feel for Miriam because I see so much of myself in her. The mouth is one of the biggest areas of potential downfall for those who hear from God regularly. Because our mouth is what the Lord uses, it can be the place the enemy attacks. Scripture makes it clear that the enemy comes to kill, steal, and destroy (John 10:10). Our area of gifting is no exception.

When I think about how my mouth gets me in trouble, I see two pitfalls. The first is not recognizing that not everything is for everyone. What I mean is that sometimes God gives me a confirmation about something, a word or insight, and it's meant for me. The temptation can be, however, to share it with other people. But sometimes a word from God is meant to be *to* us and not *through* us.

Do you see the distinction here?

If God has a personal word for us, it may just be for us—to encourage, empower, or equip us for something specific to our own lives. It is similar to how certain conversations between family members are meant to stay between them—not to be shared with the general public. There is some nuance to understanding this, but it is best to hold something close to your heart until God has made it clear that it's the appropriate time for you to share. Sometimes our sensitivity to God's leading in the timing will make a difference in the impact our words make.

The second way that is so easy for me to struggle may be common for you as well. That is the area of complaining.

One of the things I was taught as a teen is that God inhabits the praises of His people. That is 100 percent true. But the thing that most of us miss is the opposite of that statement. If God inhabits the praises of His people, who inhabits their complaints?

If God inhabits the praises of His people, who inhabits their complaints?

I know. Heavy. My goal is not to make you feel guilty. My goal is to help you realize that there are consequences to our words—both good and bad consequences.

Like Miriam leading the women in a song of praise after the Israelites crossed the Red Sea, we can invite those around us to praise. But also like Miriam, we can allow the enemy to occupy space in our words. There is tremendous power in our words. Power to bless and power to curse. Power to heal and power to hurt. Power to praise and power to be prideful. When we complain, pride can soon take over, becoming an undercurrent that slowly pulls us under.

Complaining is something we all do. It can even be something that helps people feel bonded together. It's not just socially accepted but often expected, even within the church.

The problem?

God hears our complaints.

Miriam's complaint led to God removing her from a place of influence and leadership. I don't know about you, but I don't want that kind of consequence in my life. Instead, I want to have the kind of relationship that Moses had with God—the God who knew his heart and is always listening. In Numbers 12:7, God says of Moses, "But not with my servant Moses. Of all my house, he is the one I trust" (NLT).

I want to be someone God trusts. And I believe the key is humility. Humility means understanding that any gifting from God is exactly that—a gift. Humility means realizing we are not entitled to anything. Humility means trusting the leaders God sees fit to put in spiritual authority over us. And humility means praying for those who criticize us.

If the humility of Moses was the key to remaining in God's presence, then we can see that pride is the key to Him removing it. And when God removes His hand of favor, there are consequences to not only us but also those around us. We have to be sensitive to and aware of the temptation to have a critical spirit because a critical spirit is rooted in pride. And let me be clear: This isn't about perfection. Moses wasn't perfect; he was humble. When he messed up, he came before God, asking Him for forgiveness.

That leads to our last lesson from the story of Miriam.

4. God forgives, but there are still consequences.

This is an area that actually makes a lot of sense to me as a parent. When one of my children messes up, of course I forgive them because I love them. But forgiveness doesn't mean they don't get disciplined. In fact, they get disciplined *because* I love them. God is not unlike us in that way. He is not just a Father but a *good* Father. A good Father who loves and disciplines His children.

After Miriam sins, she is forgiven, but she still must remain separated from her community for a time before she is restored to right relationship. After this incident, we don't hear of Miriam again. She doesn't enter the promised land—instead, she dies in the wilderness.

Miriam is remembered in Scripture as a woman who helped lead Israel and spoke for God to the people of God. God, in His grace, forgave her, and to this day she is seen as a woman who showed extraordinary leadership in a time when most of the leaders were men.

If Miriam can mess up, it should be clear by now that we can too. That's kind of the whole point. It's why we need Jesus—we can't get through any of this on our own.

As we close this section on Miriam, I want to encourage you to take some time to intentionally pray about any areas in your own heart that may be holding on to seeds of bitterness.

Is there anything you need to ask God for forgiveness for?

Is there anyone else you need to ask for forgiveness from?

If so, spend some time right now dealing with those things before they have a chance to grow.

Miriam was a watcher. You have to watch in order to see. And you have to listen in order to hear. Seeing and hearing God start with watching and listening.

Do you want to hear? Perhaps the better question is, Are you listening?

QUESTIONS TO PONDER

- How does the boldness of Miriam encourage you? Have there been times when you have been hesitant to speak up because there could be consequences?
- Do you live with the same sense of expectation that Miriam did? Are you equipped to praise God at any moment?
- How does the story of Miriam inspire you to trust God's leadership in your life? What can you learn from her example?
- In what ways do you experience or respond to feelings of jealousy or insecurity about others' roles or gifts? While we may intellectually understand that God has created us with unique roles, it's something else entirely to understand that at a heart level. Ask the Lord to help you see yourself the way He sees you.
- Have you ever thought about the question "If God inhabits the praises of His people, who inhabits their complaints?" Be honest in your reaction to that with God. If you spend a lot of time complaining, recognize what spirit you may be inviting into your life. If you need to, lay that down before the Lord.
- Have you ever experienced the consequences of pride, gossip, or slander in your own life? How did it affect your relationships and community? Think about the significance of Miriam being temporarily

separated from her community. How does this illustrate the impact of our actions on our relationships with others and with God?

- What are some obstacles that may be keeping you from hearing God in your life? Sin? Pride? Fear? If you say you want to hear God's voice but aren't intentional about removing the obstacles, it will be very difficult for you to move forward in this area. Spend some time specifically naming any obstacles in your life and then surrendering them to the Lord in prayer.

Spend some time in prayer, asking God to show you ways that you can declare His word for His people. Remember, the primary way God speaks to us is through His Word—the Scriptures. If spending time in God's Word is not a regular part of your daily life, consider some ways you can integrate this discipline so that you can start to hear from God more regularly in your relationship with Him.

KNOWING GOD'S VOICE IN REAL LIFE

God Cares About Your Asphalt

Years ago, I owned a Christian day care. We were located on a busy road, and there was one main door where the children were dropped off every day. Because we live in Pennsylvania, there is a lot of snow and ice every year as well as salt that is put down on the roads. Like with many of the roads all over Pennsylvania, the asphalt started to degrade in that spot over time. What started as a small hole eventually became a pothole so big that we had to put traffic cones around it after one of the parents got stuck.

This hole was in an inconvenient spot, because it was right where the children needed to be dropped off. However, my finances were not in a place where I could afford the thousands of dollars it would take to repair the driveway. In fact, at the time I couldn't even afford gravel to fill it in.

In my office, I had a whiteboard that I used to keep track of deadlines and things that were ongoing with the day care. In large letters, I wrote the word "asphalt," partly because this was a major problem I needed to figure out and partly because this was something I decided to start praying about. I didn't have the ability to take care of the asphalt, but I trusted that God did. Every day I stared at that word, praying about my driveway. I didn't know how

God was going to take care of it, but I knew that He would. So I just kept praying.

One day, about two weeks later, the doorbell rang during naptime. At first, I was incredibly upset because ringing the doorbell during naptime at a day care means that very quickly we will have lots of upset children. When I went to open the door, I saw a man covered head to toe in black smudges. Cautiously, I opened the door, thinking he must be lost.

However, my concern quickly changed to shock as this man explained that he owned a paving company. The company had been working down the road, and he had leftover asphalt. He wondered if I would let him dump the asphalt in my driveway because he could see the hole in front of the door. He even offered to bring his large rolling machine afterward to smooth it all out. Through the tears that were quickly welling up in my eyes, I gave him permission.

As I walked back into my office, my eyes immediately went to the whiteboard, where I had written the word "asphalt." God was so faithful! In a season when I was working as hard as I could, trying to be faithful with all He had given me, He showed up in a way I never thought possible. He knew exactly what I needed, and He sent it.

What does this situation have to do with hearing God's voice? Well, at that time in my life, I had no idea what prophecy even was. But I believe that operating within this spiritual gift starts long before the first day we hear God's voice. It starts with trusting God for things that only He can provide. It starts with developing a relationship with Him and being confident that He is there and that He is good. As I look back on that time in my life, a season when I needed God, I see the beginning stages of learning how to trust Him. As we learn to trust God with tangible things in our lives, we learn that He is trustworthy. When we know that He is trustworthy, we realize that He means what He says. We don't doubt it, for us or for others.

Friend, have you started trusting God with the tangible needs in your life? He longs to be in that space with you. It's time to invite Him in.

PART 2

DEBORAH

SIX

A Countercultural Identity

After we leave the story of Miriam, Moses, and Aaron, we reach a period of history when the Israelite people eventually enter the promised land. They are no longer a nomadic people wandering in the desert. They are now a people living in the land that God had promised their ancestors. Each of the twelve tribes occupies a specific area (see fig. 6.1).

There is a significant amount of time between when the Israelites enter the promised land and when they have a monarchy or a king. Depending on the date we use for the exodus (when they left Egypt), this could be between one hundred and four hundred years. During this time, the tribes govern themselves with clan leaders and elders, and God raises up leaders for specific reasons and specific seasons.

These leaders are called judges. They aren't the kinds of judges we might encounter today. Instead, they are essentially military leaders or chiefs of a tribe. They handle

Figure 6.1 **Israel Map**

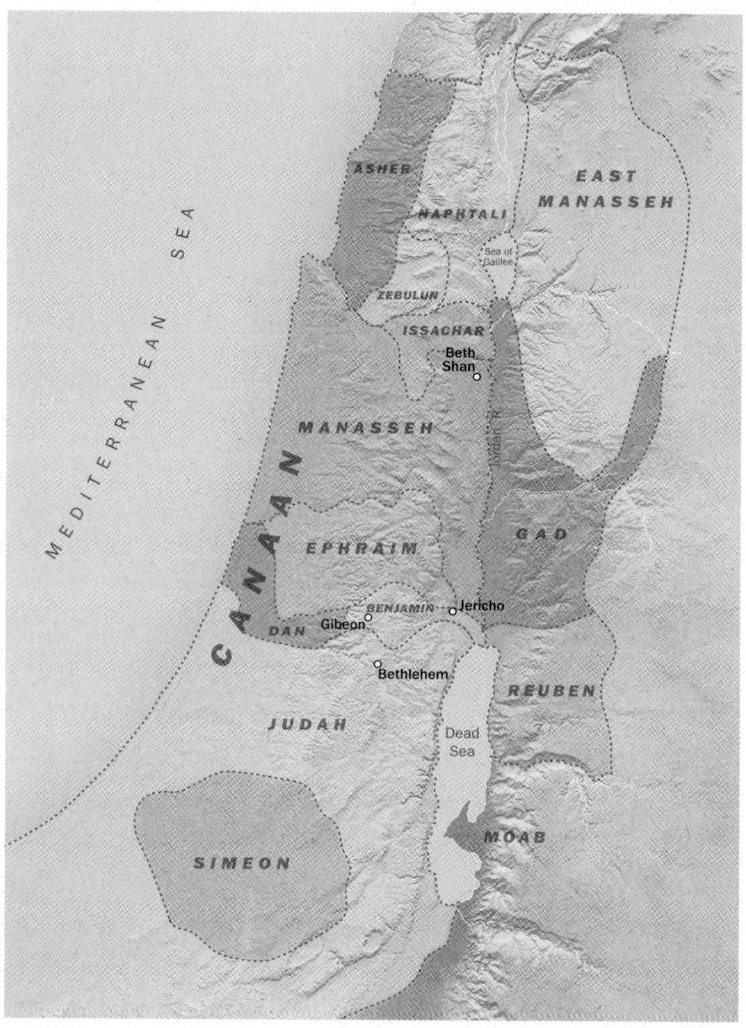

political issues, make decisions, and defend the people. These leaders are not voted on; rather, God appoints someone He deems fitting for a season. In all, there are twelve judges during this time, eleven of them men, and one of them a woman. The woman's name is Deborah, and we learn about her story in Judges 4 and 5.

While we are primarily studying the biblical record, this period in Israel's history actually happened, and there are historical records apart from the Bible that reinforce and validate what we learn from the Bible. My point is that Deborah *actually* lived and *actually* ruled over Israel. She isn't a legendary figure someone made up. There is documented evidence for her role in history.

There are many things we could study in the book of Judges, but we are going to focus on Deborah and her story because Deborah was not only a judge but also, like Miriam, a prophetess. A female leader in Israel. Set apart to help the people of God hear the words of God. Sound familiar? Let's dive in.

> Then the sons of Israel again did evil in the sight of the Lord, after Ehud died. So the Lord sold them into the hand of Jabin king of Canaan, who reigned in Hazor; and the commander of his army was Sisera, who lived in Harosheth-hagoyim. The sons of Israel cried out to the Lord; for he had nine hundred iron chariots, and he oppressed the sons of Israel severely for twenty years. (Judg. 4:1–3 NASB)

At this point in history, the Israelites were not the only people in the land of Canaan. While they considered Canaan the promised land, it took some work for them to occupy it. They did conquer much of the land, but that did not mean that everyone who was there was immediately gone. In fact, the people who remained in Canaan caused a lot of problems for the Israelites. In many cases, the people of Israel forgot about the God who had delivered them from Egypt and started worshiping other gods—the gods of the people of Canaan. While we won't get into all of that right now, it's important to understand that the people of Israel continued to disobey God in many ways.

As we saw with the story of Miriam, God allows people to suffer the consequences of their decisions. That is exactly what happens throughout the book of Judges. As this chapter opens, the people have again disobeyed God, so He allows them to fall into the hands of King Jabin. King Jabin is a leader in nearby Hazor, and he oppresses the people of Israel for more than twenty years. The leader of Jabin's army is a man named Sisera, who becomes a major player in the story of Deborah.

> Now Deborah, a prophetess, the wife of Lappidoth, was judging Israel at that time. She used to sit under the palm tree of Deborah between Ramah and Bethel in the hill country of Ephraim; and the sons of Israel went up to her for judgment. (Judg. 4:4–5 NASB)

One of the things I love about Deborah is that she, like most women, wore many hats. So many women share the same experience of being a wife, a mom, a friend, a sister, an employee, a leader, a follower—often all on the same day! It can be exhausting when we think about all the various things we are juggling, yet this is something that has been part of the human experience since the beginning of time. The problem comes when we start to lean on those roles to define our identity. While these distinct yet interdependent roles make up aspects of our personality and relationships, they can't become who we are. Our identity must be found in Jesus. Our most important role is who we are in Christ.

As we try to connect with Deborah, it may be helpful to start with the basics. Who was she? Well, the name Deborah, in Hebrew, means "honey bee."[1] But this bee was more of a worker bee than a queen bee. Despite being a woman in leadership, she was not born into royalty. She didn't seem to have any kind of extraordinary background but instead was someone like you and me.

Our identity must be found in Jesus. Our most important role is who we are in Christ.

Part of what makes Deborah so encouraging to study is that she was a normal person, with a normal name. She had normal roles within her culture, including being someone's wife. We know nothing about her husband, which shows she did not gain a position of leadership simply by being married to him. She was not handed her role as a leader in Israel by the men in her life.

While we don't know exactly how Deborah came to be in a position of leadership, we do know that it was quite countercultural for the time. During a time when Israel was a patriarchal society, the very fact that Deborah held the role that she did is evidence of her extraordinary leadership skills. Deborah was chosen by God to speak on behalf of God in a time when that simply was not typical. The rest of the judges of Israel were male. The entire monarchy in Israel was male. We do see women being used by God throughout the Old and New Testaments, but none had quite the leadership role that Deborah did.

Some scholars believe the name Deborah comes from a root word that means "to lead or to pursue."[2] In the ancient world, a lot of significance was placed on someone's name. It often reflected their character, personality, and behavior. So Deborah's name signifies that her leadership character trait likely existed long before she was leading as a judge.

Understanding someone's name may seem like a small detail that we might otherwise skip over, but I think there is something else for us to gain if we linger here for a moment longer. As I was researching the life of Deborah, I came across something incredibly interesting. Deborah's name is actually a Hebrew anagram of the words "she spoke."[3] An anagram, for those of us who don't remember, is a word or phrase made by transposing the letters of another word or phrase. If we look at the name of Deborah with that in mind, then it seems that the most likely interpretation of her name would actually be "to lead or pursue," because it is consistent with how we see her name presented in Scripture. This showcases Deborah's role in Israel and how God used her for His purposes. Deborah was used by God as a leader who spoke on His behalf.

One additional insight. Deborah was called the "wife of Lappidoth," which translates to "a fiery woman."[4]

Deborah the prophetess, wife, and judge.

Worker bee.

To lead or to pursue.

She spoke.

Fiery woman.

Does this sound like someone you want to get to know? Me too.

SEVEN

A Woman of Influence

> Now [Deborah] sent word and summoned Barak the son of Abinoam from Kedesh-naphtali, and said to him, "The Lord, the God of Israel, has indeed commanded, 'Go and march to Mount Tabor, and take with you ten thousand men from the sons of Naphtali and from the sons of Zebulun. I will draw out to you Sisera, the commander of Jabin's army, with his chariots and his many troops to the river Kishon, and I will hand him over to you.'" Then Barak said to her, "If you will go with me, then I will go; but if you will not go with me, I will not go." She said, "I will certainly go with you; however, the fame shall not be yours on the journey that you are about to take, for the Lord will sell Sisera into the hand of a woman." Then Deborah got up and went with Barak to Kedesh. Barak summoned Zebulun and Naphtali to Kedesh, and ten thousand men went up with him; Deborah also went up with him. (Judg. 4:6–10 NASB)

As you can probably imagine, after being oppressed by King Jabin for twenty years, the Israelites turn to the Lord for help.

In answer to their prayers, God speaks through Deborah. We have already established that Deborah was a leader, but we start to see the roles of judge and prophet showcased in this part of Israel's history.

Both as a judge and as a prophet, Deborah was equipped by God to lead His people. Her close relationship with God enabled her to have great influence among her people. She was already working within her calling when God placed her in leadership. Her obedience in the smaller things is what led to God trusting her with the bigger things. When I think back over my life, I see areas where this was true for me as well. Perhaps you do too.

No one saw the pain I endured as a child. But God did.

No one saw the brokenness I lived in when I was in an abusive marriage. But God did.

No one saw the countless hours of therapy I went through as I healed. But God did.

No one saw the conversations I had with young mothers as they picked up their children from the church nursery. But God did.

No one saw the late nights I spent writing papers during seminary. But God did.

No one saw the heartache and tears as the child we had spent five years trying to adopt was trafficked to another country. But God did.

No one heard the harsh words spoken to me by toxic "Christian" leaders. But God did.

He heard. He saw. And He used those moments to mold me into the leader I am today. Despite it all, I continued to serve Him faithfully among the people He gave me influence over. In each of those moments, God was preparing me for the people He has called me to serve today.

I don't believe the prophecy and leadership we see in Deborah started suddenly when there was a need. Deborah had already been serving in that community. She had already been using the gifts God had given her to serve Him. She was already in a place to be used by God when the need arose.

Her obedience in the smaller things is what led to God trusting her with the bigger things.

I think that's key for us. We need to practice hearing God's voice in the day-to-day. In our jobs, in our marriages, in our communities. God will help us grow spiritually and give us gifts as we are faithful in what He gives us today.

Deborah sat under the palm tree of Deborah as she served her community. Some scholars think this was a physical location, while others think it was more her overall presence within the daily lives of the people she served. In the ancient world, the palm tree was seen as a metaphor for growth and leadership. The palm tree was an important part of the landscape, offering shelter and provision. It was a valued part of their daily lives. Whether the palm tree of Deborah was a physical location or a metaphorical one, it is clear that Deborah became synonymous with that place within her community.

Deborah was serving God with the gifts He had given her—as a leader, as a judge, and as a prophet. If we are wanting God to use us, to work through us, then we must start by being faithful with what He has given us today. The blessings of tomorrow are birthed in the obedience of today.

◆◆◆

Deborah is involved in her community as a leader, taking seriously the pain of her people. When the Lord directs her, she sends for a man named Barak, who is from the tribe named Naphtali. Deborah shares the military strategy the Lord has given her to recruit ten thousand men from the tribes of Naphtali and Zebulun. This likely represented many more than ten thousand because, in the ancient world, this was similar to how Americans use the term "a million" today. She was essentially telling him to get a huge number of guys to get ready to fight. Then God will lure Sisera and his army to the river, where God will give Barak and his men victory.

Barak is on board but only barely. He agrees on one condition: Deborah must go with him. Perhaps he is afraid. Or perhaps he doesn't think the men will listen to this crazy idea unless Deborah is the one saying it. Or perhaps her leadership is what will give him the confidence to fight such an intimidating battle.

Deborah has already assured Barak that God promises victory for Israel, but she agrees to go with him, warning him that he will lose the honor that would normally come with capturing Sisera. In a culture where women were not valued like they are today, the credit for defeating the general and the Canaanite army will go to a woman. Barak seems to agree that he doesn't need the glory, because he and Deborah set off together to recruit the men. They get everything in place the way God said, postured for battle.

We see very plainly from her interaction with Barak that Deborah is in a unique position when it comes time to deal with a crisis. She handles it with the authority of one who has a direct connection with Yahweh—the God of Israel.

The reason we see Deborah respond the way she does is because of her confidence in her relationship with God. That relationship did not start the day the crisis came. It started long before and was fostered as she obediently served Him in the day-to-day.

If our goal is to hear God's voice more clearly, we must start listening within the rhythm of our daily lives, not when the crisis hits. We must listen in the days that are filled with washing dishes and filling out spreadsheets. In the quiet moments between worship songs. In the frustrations of politics and inflation and illness. We must cultivate a relationship with God that is real. We must be good stewards of the small things God gives us before He will trust us with the big things. This is exactly what Deborah did so that when it was time to rally the troops, they came. They knew she was trustworthy because they had seen her leadership, character, and relationship with God tested over time.

◆◆◆

I know there isn't a lot of teaching on the women of Scripture who are referred to as prophets. It's part of the reason I decided to write about this topic. Let's unpack it a little bit because I want you to realize that "hearing from God" isn't reserved for specific people today like it was in the Old Testament. As followers of Jesus, we all have access to the Holy Spirit. He is the one who enables and empowers us to hear His voice more clearly.

In the Old Testament, the word that refers to a prophet is *nabi*. It is often translated as "a spokesman or a speaker for God."[1] During the time that Deborah lived, there often was a specific person within a community who was called a prophet or a prophetess because they were chosen servants who could speak on God's behalf through a gifting of God. Deborah was called a *nabi*. In her role, Deborah revealed the direction and wisdom of God as she served as an advisor and judge to her people. God clearly does not discriminate between men and women when it comes to leadership and gifting—even if people do. As we continue to learn about various women throughout this book, it's important for us to remember this. The Bible states:

> And it shall come to pass afterward,
> that I will pour out my Spirit on all flesh;
> your sons and your daughters shall prophesy,
> your old men shall dream dreams,
> and your young men shall see visions. (Joel 2:28 ESV)

It's time we stop disqualifying ourselves from being used by God because we don't think He will use us. God does not discriminate when it comes to who He uses. He does not disqualify us based on our age, our position, or our gender.

Let me say that again for those in the back of the room: God does not discriminate when it comes to who He uses. Why do we?

EIGHT

A Trusted Voice for the Lord

Now Heber the Kenite had separated himself from the Kenites, from the sons of Hobab the father-in-law of Moses, and had pitched his tent as far away as the oak in Zaanannim, which is near Kedesh.

Then they told Sisera that Barak the son of Abinoam had gone up to Mount Tabor. Sisera summoned all his chariots, nine hundred iron chariots, and all the people who were with him, from Harosheth-hagoyim to the river Kishon. Then Deborah said to Barak, "Arise! For this is the day on which the Lord has handed Sisera over to you; behold, the Lord has gone out before you." So Barak went down from Mount Tabor with ten thousand men following him. And the Lord routed Sisera and all his chariots and all his army with the edge of the sword before Barak; and Sisera got down from his chariot and fled on foot. But Barak pursued the chariots and the army as far as Harosheth-hagoyim, and all the army of Sisera fell by the edge of the sword; not even one was left. (Judg. 4:11–16 NASB)

Heber the Kenite separated himself from the Kenites. What does that have to do with anything? Well, remember Moses's wife, Zipporah? The one Miriam criticized him for marrying? Her family was Kenite. Zipporah's father was Jethro, one of the Kenites. They were friendly to the people of Israel, at least friendly enough for Moses to marry one of them. But Heber? Not so much. He deliberately distanced himself from his people. So Heber is no longer an ally of Israel. Instead, he is an ally of the enemy of Israel in this story, King Jabin. That will become important later in the story, but I wanted to mention it here so we didn't skip right over it.

When Sisera, who works for King Jabin, learns about the Israelite army that Deborah and Barak have gathered, he orders his nine hundred iron chariots and soldiers to head to Mount Tabor to fight them. But the way he sends them shows a lot of arrogance on his part. The direction he sends the troops gives Israel the advantage because of their position. We can tell from this decision that Sisera doesn't really take the Israelites seriously, thinking he can beat them easily.

What happens next is a testimony to Deborah's wisdom and strategy, which the Lord had given her. Deborah gives the order to attack Sisera's army, and the Israelites easily defeat them. Sisera runs away on foot, but the rest of them die, every last one of them. This was incredibly rare in ancient times. It was more typical that some would die, one side would retreat, and so on. But in this case, the Israelites defeat King Jabin's army thoroughly. This means that King Jabin will no longer have power over them.

At this point in Israel's history, they did not have a strong military. They did not have the right weapons or equipment to fight the kind of army that would have nine hundred chariots. How did Deborah convince Barak and the men of Israel to rise up and fight such a dangerous enemy? How did she get them to risk their lives in battle?

Deborah had proven herself over time, in all the moments leading up to this moment. They trusted her. This is the evidence of a life that was lived faithfully. Her word was proven to be trustworthy over and over again.

Sometimes the Lord intervenes, giving us a new gift as the opportunity to use it arises. But more often gifts grow in us over time. God gives us opportunities to steward the small things well before He trusts us with the big things. Even though Deborah was asking Barak and the men of Israel to fight against a powerful army that they weren't equipped to fight, they knew they could trust her. If God told her to do this, then they would do it. They trusted Deborah, and Deborah trusted God.

Deborah was a woman of influence who used her voice for the Lord. God used her to lead the entire nation into victory. God used her to deliver the people of Israel from the hands of their oppressors. Despite cultural limitations and expectations, God used a woman to accomplish His plan and purpose. He still does this today. God still uses women to lead, using the gifts He gives.

In this story of Deborah being used as God's vessel and agent, we see a couple things that I want to make sure we don't miss.

Deborah's role as a prophet was what enabled her to lead the people. It was her relationship with God that gave her the wisdom, vision, and words that He would use to rescue the people of Israel, even though the role of the prophet was usually reserved for men. God cares more about your heart and your relationship with Him than He does about societal expectations. There is not a different version of the Holy Spirit for women than there is for men. We all have access to Him—to hear His voice and to be used by Him. God does not discriminate between genders when He empowers people for His glory and His plans. He is not necessarily looking for a man to lead. He is looking for a heart that is open to being led.

God cares more about your heart and your relationship with Him than He does about societal expectations.

In Deborah's case, her prophetic gift cannot be separated from her role as judge. That often is how it works for us too. If you are willing not just to listen to God but also to speak for Him and obey Him, then it is likely that you will be given a role of leadership. God is looking for leaders, especially in the cultural climate we live in. In Deborah's time, that leadership looked like being a judge. As she offered spiritual, religious, and practical leadership to her community, God developed gifts in her that He would eventually use in a way that He saw fit. In the daily use of those gifts, God continued to refine her, making her more attuned to His voice.

Her character and reputation, which were tested over time, were the very reasons that Barak trusted her when she laid out the plan for battle. Taking that one step further, Barak had the confidence to go only if Deborah went with him. Perhaps he felt that she had the connection to God and that connection was the only way they could win. But Barak failed to recognize that he could trust God, which led to some consequences.

> "Certainly, I will go with you," said Deborah. "But because of the course you are taking, the honor will not be yours, for the Lord will deliver Sisera into the hands of a woman." So Deborah went with Barak to Kedesh. (Judg. 4:9)

Deborah reminds Barak that Yahweh Himself is the one in control, giving direction and strategy. This reminder gives Barak the courage to step out in faith as he advances the Israelites toward Sisera's army. Deborah's words are a source of strength in his time of doubt.

We are living in a world that is full of doubt. God is looking for people who will remind the body of Christ what God has already said and the authority He has already given us as His children—especially in times of doubt.

If we set aside nonbelievers for a moment and consider only believers, there is still a lot of insecurity around how to live in a world that is so blatant with sin. People who have been believers for a long time still struggle with how to talk to their coworkers, their neighbors, or even their family members about God. The reason for this?

People often know *about* God without really *knowing* God.

Friend, we have to do something about this. It is our role *to know Him and to make Him known.*

Deborah asks Barak a rhetorical question to help him remember that he is not going alone, to remind Barak of what God has already said: "Has not the Lord gone ahead of you?"

(Judg. 4:14). That so often is the role of a prophet. To remind the people of God of the words of God.

There have been so many times in my life when I forgot what God has said. Or maybe I didn't forget so much as I doubted.

Can God *really* do what He said He will do?

Does God *really* keep His promises?

Can I *really* do the thing He has called me to do?

Would God *really* choose to use me?

The truth is all of us need people in our lives who remind us of what God has already said. Whether it was a word that God gave us personally or a promise that we read in His Word, sometimes we need to be reminded of it.

Who are the people in your life God has called you to lead? They're probably not an army. Maybe they're your coworkers. Or your children. Or people in your church. The bottom line? Don't hesitate to use your voice to remind the people of God of the words of God.

NINE

The Prophecy Fulfilled

At this point, you may be wondering what happened to Sisera. We learned that all of King Jabin's army died, but Sisera ran away like a little baby. Well, eventually Sisera comes to the home of Heber. Remember how I pointed out that Heber had left his people and was no longer an ally of the Israelites? Heber was actually on King Jabin's side. That's why Sisera thinks it's safe to take shelter there. He expects some help or, at the very least, a place to hide while he catches his breath.

Heber is married to a woman named Jael, and she invites Sisera into their tent. She gives him some milk and a place to sleep and assures him that she will keep watch for anyone who may be following him. Interestingly enough, it was a cultural expectation at the time that the owner of a home would protect a guest, so Sisera likely felt safe enough to drift off to sleep.

What happens next is a fulfillment of the prophecy Deborah told Barak. Once Sisera falls asleep, Jael picks up a hammer and a tent peg, which was basically a sharp wooden spike. She drives the spike into the soft part on the side of Sisera's head, pinning his skull to the ground. Sisera is dead, defeated by a woman. Just like Deborah said he would be. The prophecy of Deborah is fulfilled. Deborah may have been the commander-in-chief, but Jael was the assassin that finished the job.

Let's review the account in Judges 4:17–24:

> Now Sisera fled on foot to the tent of Jael the wife of Heber the Kenite, because there was peace between Jabin the king of Hazor and the house of Heber the Kenite. And Jael went out to meet Sisera, and said to him, "Turn aside, my master, turn aside to me! Do not be afraid." So he turned aside to her into the tent, and she covered him with a rug. And he said to her, "Please give me a little water to drink, for I am thirsty." So she opened a leather bottle of milk and gave him a drink; then she covered him. And he said to her, "Stand in the doorway of the tent, and it shall be if anyone comes and inquires of you, and says, 'Is there anyone here?' that you shall say, 'No.'" But Jael, Heber's wife, took a tent peg and a hammer in her hand, and went secretly to him and drove the peg into his temple, and it went through into the ground; for he was sound asleep and exhausted. So he died. And behold, while Barak was pursuing Sisera, Jael came out to meet him and said to him, "Come, and I will show you the man whom you are seeking." So he entered with her, and behold, Sisera was lying dead with the tent peg in his temple.
>
> So God subdued Jabin the king of Canaan on that day before the sons of Israel. And the hand of the sons of Israel pressed harder and harder upon Jabin the king of Canaan, until they had eliminated Jabin the king of Canaan. (NASB)

Even though Barak is the military leader in the story, he loses the honor he normally would have had because of his reluctance to follow God's plan. He insisted Deborah go with him. Because of this, Jael is the one who achieves the victory by finishing off Sisera.

Does this story surprise you at all? Jael was a foreigner; she wasn't even an Israelite. We never learn her motives. It's possible that she remained loyal in her heart to the people of Israel even though her husband did not. Maybe she just didn't like Sisera; he was known to be cruel and oppressive as the general for King Jabin. Maybe she knew that it was obviously the hand of Yahweh that gave Israel such an impressive defeat of such a powerful army. Regardless of the reason, Jael completes what Deborah started, and we see God use two women to accomplish His plan. With his army gone, it's not long before King Jabin is taken out, and Israel is no longer under his oppressive rule.

What happens next is similar to what we saw with Miriam: Deborah responds with a song of praise and worship. As we noted earlier, there is a strong connection between a heart of worship and a heart that regularly hears from the Lord. Deborah and Barak both sing a song that praises God for what they went through. It celebrates the defeat of Jabin's army and proudly declares that God is the God of victory—He is responsible for giving them freedom from their oppressors.

After you read the song they sang, spend some time in prayer, rehearsing any areas of victory in your own life. Perhaps God used you in a powerful way to intervene in a certain situation. But don't forget the One who enabled that to happen in the first place: Yahweh. He is always the one who brings the victory.

The Victory Song of Deborah and Barak

Blessings be to Yahweh,
who gave us victory today!
For the people answered the call,
and Israel threw off what once held us back.
Listen, you kings!
Open your ears, you princes!
For I will sing a song to Yahweh.
I will make music to Yahweh, the God of Israel.
Yahweh, when you advanced from Seir,
and when you marched from Edom's plains,
the earth trembled,
the sky poured,
the clouds burst,
and the mountains melted,
in the presence of Yahweh, the *Glorious* One of Sinai,
in the presence of Yahweh, the God of Israel!
In the days of Shamgar son of Anath,
and in the days of Jael, *no one felt safe*;
the roads were deserted,
and those who *dared to* travel took back roads.
Champions were hard to find—
hard to find in Israel,
until I, Deborah, took a stand!
I arose as a mother in Israel!
The Israelites chose new gods,
which brought war into the land.
Of forty thousand men in Israel,
not a shield or spear was seen.
My heart is with Israel's princes,
with the people who gladly volunteered.
Praise Yahweh!

Declare it, you *rich*
who ride on your white donkeys,
sitting on your *fancy* saddles!
Declare it, you *poor*
who must walk wherever you go!
Listen to the sound of singers at the well,
as they proclaim the victories of Yahweh,
the righteous triumph of his villagers in Israel!
Then the people of Yahweh
marched out from their city gates!
Lead on, O Deborah, lead on!
Awake, awake! Break out in a song!
Arise, O Barak, arise!
Son of Abinoam, arise!
Carry off your captives
and lead them all away!
The remaining nobles marched out,
Yahweh's people came to me to fight against the
mighty ones.
You men of Ephraim came out to the valley,
your brother Benjamin joined your ranks.
Leaders came from Manasseh,
and from Zebulun, those who hold the ruler's staff.
Issachar's princes rallied to Deborah,
Issachar stood fast alongside Barak,
rushing into the valley under Barak's command,
while among Reuben's clans there was great
searching of heart.
Reuben, why do you remain by the sheepfolds,
listening for the shepherds to whistle for their flocks?
Among Reuben's clans there was great searching of
heart.

Gad *played it safe and* stayed east of the Jordan,
and Dan lingered near their ships,
while Asher kept their distance and stayed by the coast,
safe and secure in their harbors.
But Zebulun and Naphtali defied death
and risked it all on the heights of the battlefield.
At Taanach foreign kings came and clashed;
they battled by the stream of Megiddo.
The kings of Canaan fought,
but they took away no spoils of silver.
Even the stars in the sky joined in the fight,
moving across the sky,
shining as they fought against Sisera.
The flooding Kishon swept them away—
the ancient Kishon River *contended with them*.
I shall march and keep marching on.
So be strong, O my soul!
Then thundered the horses' hooves, *pulling the chariots of the kings of Canaan.*
Here they come galloping on,
steeds and stallions stampeding on,
but they all got stuck in the mud!
"Speak a curse over Meroz," says the angel of Yahweh,
"and speak a double curse over those who live there.
For they did not come to help Yahweh's cause
nor rally to Yahweh's side to fight the mighty."
The most blessed of all women is Jael,
wife of Heber the Kenite—
the most fortunate of Bedouin women.
Sisera *came to Jael's tent and* asked for water,
but she gave him milk;
she brought him buttermilk in a beautiful bowl.

With a tent peg in one hand
and a workman's hammer in the other,
she struck Sisera and pierced his skull;
she drove the peg through his temple.
She shattered his skull,
and he lay still before Jael.
Sprawled on the tent floor,
he bit the dust at her feet—
deader than a doornail!
Sisera's mother waited for him at her window;
she gazed from behind the lattice and lamented:
"Why is the clatter of his chariot so late in coming?
Why are his horses so slow to return?"
The wisest of her princesses replied;
indeed, she even thought to herself:
"They must be gathering and dividing the spoils:
a slave-girl or two for each man,
colorful cloth and garments as plunder for Sisera,
two colorful garments, embroidered,
and richly embroidered garments for my neck."
YAHWEH, may all who hate you perish in the same way!
But may those who love you shine like the sun,
bright in its strength as it crosses the sky!

Then the land had peace for forty years. (Judg. 5:2–31 TPT)

TEN

How to Be Like Deborah

When we consider the story of Deborah and Barak, we see some similarities to the way God operated when He intervened on behalf of the Israelites in the story of Miriam and Moses. One of the things we learn in Deborah's victory song is that God used nature to work in their favor: "The flooding Kishon swept them away—the ancient Kishon River *contended with them*" (Judg. 5:21 TPT). The Kishon River ran through the area, and part of it swelled with a torrent, sweeping away the army. The mud would have trapped their chariots. God used a natural phenomenon to help fight Israel's oppressors.

Sound familiar?

Despite the fact that not all the tribes of Israel helped in the battle . . . despite the fact that the guy who should have been leading the charge was afraid to do it alone . . . despite the fact that the Israelites didn't have the right kind of weapons . . . despite the fact that untrained people were up against a trained army . . . despite the fact that all of this was being led by a woman . . . we see a God who shows up. A God who shows up in a miraculous way that no one could have predicted. Deborah likely didn't know exactly how God was going to do what He said He would do. She just knew that He would.

That is the mark of a woman who can be used by God. Absolute trust that the one who says He will *actually* will. But first we have to learn to recognize the voice of God in our lives. How do we do that?

Through God's Word. God's Word teaches us to recognize His voice. That may seem like the Sunday school answer, but it is 100 percent the truth. There is no special prayer, no perfect formula. Learning to recognize God's voice comes from reading His Word. Period. If you aren't willing to make reading God's Word a regular part of your daily life, then you may as well put this book down right now. I can give you all the testimonies you could ever want, tell you how God works in my life, but if you aren't willing to develop the discipline of reading His Word, there is no point to reading my words.

You have to read God's Word to be able to recognize God's voice.

You have to read God's Word to be able to recognize God's voice. Because God's voice will never contradict His Word.

Here are two additional thoughts as we wrap up the study of Deborah. The first is centered on doubt.

Barak had some doubts when it came time to actually step out in faith based on what Deborah was telling him. It's not likely that he doubted Deborah because he pleaded with her to go with him. It's more likely that he doubted God.

Eventually, he stepped forward in faith, but there was a consequence for his doubt. Doubting God robbed Barak of what God originally had in store for him. Deborah prophesied that Barak would lose honor in battle and the victory would come at the hands of a woman.

There is blessing in witnessing the victory of God in our lives, especially when God has used us as part of the process. Sometimes the enemy comes in and uses doubt to keep us from what God has for us. The lesson? Don't allow the enemy to use doubt to keep you from what God has for you.

The second point I want to make involves the opposite of doubt—it's about faith. Deborah saw a huge victory, her words of prophecy were proven true, and Israel experienced forty years of peace. But it took faith and obedience on Deborah's part to get there.

It takes a lot of faith to speak what God places on our hearts. And it takes obedience to step out and do whatever it is that God has called us to do.

Share my faith at work? Faith and obedience.

Share my testimony with someone who is struggling? Faith and obedience.

Sponsor a child in a developing country? Faith and obedience.

Go on that mission trip? Faith and obedience.

Tithe the entire 10 percent on that inheritance? Faith and obedience.

Sometimes the blessings in our lives are directly connected to the amount of faith and obedience we have.

There's a caveat, though. We should never be obedient just because we want the blessing. Instead, living a life of obedience should be the natural by-product of a vibrant relationship with Jesus.

You may be thinking, *How do I get that kind of relationship with Jesus?*

Well, how do you get that kind of relationship with anyone? Your spouse? Your dad? Your best friend? You get it by spending time with them. Lots of time. You *know* them. And you know that they *know* you. You know that they are trustworthy and are going to be there for you. (Assuming these are healthy relationships.) Your trust of someone is birthed out of spending time with them and the consistency they show you over the course of the relationship. The same is true in our relationship with God. We know Him by spending time with Him. We recognize His voice over time. Once we get to that place, He is really hard to ignore.

Trust me, I've tried.

QUESTIONS TO PONDER

- Deborah wore many hats, including being a wife and a leader. Her story demonstrates that people who start off leading ordinary lives can be used by God in extraordinary ways when their identity is rooted in who God says they are. How can you remain open to God's calling in your everyday life even when it seems ordinary?
- Deborah's obedience in small things led to greater responsibilities within the kingdom of Israel. How can you practice faithfulness in your daily life to prepare for God's bigger plans? Realize that your stewardship of the small things will determine your ability to receive the bigger things.
- Deborah's leadership was recognized because of her proven character. How can you build trust and credibility in your own community or workplace? Remember that your character is determined not just by your words but by who you are when no one else is looking.
- How do you reconcile moments of fear or hesitation with the need to trust in God's sovereignty and plan? Have you ever experienced a moment when you had to trust God's plan without knowing how it would unfold? How did you respond?
- Think about your own experiences with faith and obedience. How have they shaped your relationship

with God and your ability to hear His voice? Remember that delayed obedience is disobedience. How can you hold yourself accountable to quick obedience?

Spend some time in prayer, reflecting on ways you can grow in both faith and obedience to deepen your relationship with God. Ask Him for opportunities to exercise faith and the strength to be obedient when those opportunities arise.

KNOWING GOD'S VOICE IN REAL LIFE

When You Refuse to Listen

I was volunteering in New York City with a group I had worked with for years. It was one of my favorite weeks of the year, helping busloads of kids enter the ministry center to hear the gospel. I had taken a team of about twenty volunteers with me, and we were helping guide kids in and get seated. The room was buzzing with anticipation. Balloons were on the stage, killer prizes were stacked in the corner, and hundreds of kids were lining the bleachers. It was going to be a good day. Excited about the cute preschoolers sitting in front of me, I initially tried to dismiss the voice that I heard in my heart.

Go sit by her.

I knew exactly who He was talking about. An older girl, probably around twelve or so, had just walked past me. I had to hold my breath as she walked by because she smelled so bad. I averted my eyes, uncomfortable in the situation, and did my best to ignore her. Even though I wouldn't have admitted it out loud, a part of me was relieved when she kept walking instead of taking the empty seat near me.

Go sit by her.

The excuses kept coming.

It was my brain playing tricks on me.

As a mama, I was just feeling bad for her.

Someone else was going to sit by her any second.

Someone needed to keep an eye on these preschoolers.

Go sit by her.

It was at this point that I made the conscious decision to disobey God. I did not go sit by her. Instead, I did my best to pay attention to the event and engage the preschoolers sitting near me. I tried to trick myself into thinking I was faithfully serving where I was instead of obeying God by not going where He had called me.

As much as I tried to ignore that girl and that entire scenario, to this day I cannot get her out of my head. Why didn't I go sit by her? If you had asked me, I would have said that I went to New York City to serve however the Lord wanted me to. I would have said that I was the leader on that trip and would faithfully obey God as an example to my team. I would have said that God loves all kids—even the ones who smell bad—and I did too. I was a children's pastor at the time, and I was no stranger to kids who came from hard places. But I didn't go sit by her.

In many ways, I regret that decision. But at the same time, I don't because of the way it still weighs on my heart all these years later. I still think about that girl. I still pray for her. I still remember exactly what she looked like, what she was wearing, and the look on her face as she sat there alone.

I remember.

You know what I don't remember? I don't remember what was said that day. I don't remember the faces of the cute little preschoolers. I don't remember who won the prizes or what songs were sung.

But I remember her. I remember her any time God tells me to do something. Any time He prompts me to talk to someone, to say something, to go somewhere. I remember her. And I remember the feeling of being disobedient to God in that moment. I remember how it still feels.

That is the weight of hearing from God when we *don't* listen. I can't ignore Him now. I know better. I know how much ignoring His voice weighs. So now?

Faith and obedience.

PART 3

HULDAH

ELEVEN

The Discovery That Changed Everything

It would be very difficult to tell the story of our next female prophet, Huldah, without first telling the story of King Josiah. After the time of the judges, the period in which Deborah and Barak's story takes place, Israel had several more judges before finally getting a monarch, King Saul.

After Saul, there was a series of kings: King Ish-Bosheth, King David, and King Solomon. After Solomon's reign, the kingdom was divided into the northern (Israel) and southern (Judah) kingdoms by Solomon's sons. Each kingdom then had its own set of kings moving forward. Some of these kings were good (meaning they did right in the eyes of the Lord) and others were bad (they did evil in the eyes of the Lord).

Josiah was a king in the southern kingdom of Judah, and he was the last king of Judah who did right in the eyes of the Lord. Eventually, the kingdom of Judah fell into the hands of the Babylonians, and the people of Israel were held in captivity for seventy years.

The name Josiah means "Yahweh heals," and that is a really good indication of Josiah's heart. He sought to follow the Lord and all His commands. He took the throne at the tender age of eight after his father was murdered by his servants for being such an idolatrous leader. Josiah reigned for thirty-one years. Let's see how his reign was recorded in Scripture:

> Josiah was eight years old when he became king, and he reigned in Jerusalem thirty-one years. His mother's name was Jedidah daughter of Adaiah; she was from Bozkath. He did what was right in the eyes of the LORD and followed completely the ways of his father David, not turning aside to the right or to the left. (2 Kings 22:1–2)

One of the hallmarks of Josiah's reign is that he began to purge the kingdom of all idolatry. King Josiah pursued God and tore down all the places where the people worshiped false gods, otherwise known as "high places." While this had been done before by kings like King Hezekiah, it had never been done so thoroughly. King Josiah even burned down some of the places of idol worship in the northern kingdom, which had not been done before. By this point in history, the northern kingdom had already fallen to the Assyrian Empire. However, the Assyrians had started to lose their grip on the region a little, giving King Josiah the ability to purge areas in the north. This was unprecedented, and to this day King Josiah is known for the way he worked to restore the people of Israel to a right relationship with God.

A second thing that is significant about King Josiah is that he made it a priority to make repairs to the temple.

> In the eighteenth year of his reign, King Josiah sent the secretary, Shaphan son of Azaliah, the son of Meshullam, to the temple of the LORD. He said: "Go up to Hilkiah the high priest and have him get ready the money that has been brought into the temple of the LORD, which the doorkeepers have collected from the people. Have them entrust it to the men appointed to supervise the work on the temple. And have these men pay the workers who repair the temple of the LORD—the carpenters, the builders and the masons. Also have them purchase timber and dressed stone to repair the temple. But they need not account for the money entrusted to them, because they are honest in their dealings." (2 Kings 22:3–7)

During this time, something happened that would change the course of Josiah's reign in Judah. A book known as the "Book of the Law" was discovered by the royal priest during the temple repairs. The priest took the book to the royal scribe, who read it to King Josiah. Josiah was immediately grieved because he realized that the kingdom was not following God's law. As the leader of the nation, the weight of their disobedience was on his shoulders. For this reason, he needed to find out if this book was real.

> Hilkiah the high priest said to Shaphan the secretary, "I have found the Book of the Law in the temple of the LORD." He gave it to Shaphan, who read it. Then Shaphan the secretary went to the king and reported to him: "Your officials have paid out the money that was in the temple of the LORD and have

> entrusted it to the workers and supervisors at the temple." Then Shaphan the secretary informed the king, "Hilkiah the priest has given me a book." And Shaphan read from it in the presence of the king.
>
> When the king heard the words of the Book of the Law, he tore his robes. He gave these orders to Hilkiah the priest, Ahikam son of Shaphan, Akbor son of Micaiah, Shaphan the secretary and Asaiah the king's attendant: "Go and inquire of the LORD for me and for the people and for all Judah about what is written in this book that has been found. Great is the LORD's anger that burns against us because those who have gone before us have not obeyed the words of this book; they have not acted in accordance with all that is written there concerning us." (2 Kings 22:8–13)

The temple held significance for the ancient Near East culture. Not only was it the center of the economy but it also represented the place where God dwelt among His people. It was the duty of the monarch to make sure the temple was in good repair as a show of respect and honor to God. This had been neglected prior to King Josiah's reign, but as he sought the Lord in his leadership, he made sure to prioritize God's house. This meant not just repairing what was damaged but also removing anything unclean that had been brought inside as well as restoring it spiritually. There would be a need for ongoing finances dedicated by the kingdom coffers for the upkeep of the temple and the care of the priests who would run it.

Before we move on, I think something can be gleaned from the life of King Josiah that we have seen so far. He inherited the kingdom from a father who did not honor the

Lord. He spent a great deal of effort, time, and money undoing the damage someone else had done. The work of restoration was difficult and took a lot of intentional effort over many years. He found people skilled in restoration work to help him.

I think sometimes our own lives can be like that. We inherit things from our family that are quite a mess. Perhaps it is abuse, or poverty, or addiction. Maybe you are the first Christian in your family. Or maybe you're dealing with the chaos in the world around you without the support of those who have gone before you. Sometimes decisions made years ago impact our lives today. Often those kinds of things can leave us feeling paralyzed. King Josiah, from the very young age of eight, was charged with cleaning up his father's mess.

We can't stay stuck in the mess we inherited. We have to start climbing out.

I feel that. I feel that deep in my bones.

It's not fair.

I didn't make this mess.

I didn't ask for this.

I'm not responsible.

Insert whatever thought is going through your mind here.

Friend, I get it. I really do. But we can't stay stuck in the mess we inherited. We have to start climbing out. We need to start burning down the idols and high places in our lives one at a time. Josiah had a mountain of work cut out for him. In all likelihood, when he looked at what needed to be done and the time he had to do it, he probably felt discouraged. But you know what? He did it anyway.

You may feel unequipped. The truth is we all are. That's why we need the body of Christ. Like Josiah, who hired people skilled in restoration, we may also have to call in backup. This may mean getting help from therapists or counselors. Perhaps it means taking a class on financial responsibility and budgeting. Or maybe it means asking someone to hold you accountable in an area you struggle. That's okay. It's how God designed the church to work—people in relationship with one another. It's kind of the whole point—God is in the business of restoration. And it's a restored heart that can hear Him the most clearly.

We will continue learning about King Josiah as we move into Huldah's role in the story. But there is something I want you to realize about him in order to have the full context.

Do you remember King David? If I asked you, "Who was the most faithful king Israel ever had?" it's likely you would answer, "King David." I don't blame you. He wrote most of the Psalms. Or maybe you would answer, "King Solomon, David's son." He was the one who built the temple in the first place.

But do you know what? King Josiah is remembered as *more* faithful than any other king in Israel. More faithful than King David? Yes, you read that right. And I have the proof. Look what the Bible says just one chapter later:

> The king gave this order to all the people: "Celebrate the Passover to the LORD your God, as it is written in this Book of the Covenant." Neither in the days of the judges who led Israel nor in the days of the kings of Israel and the kings of Judah

> had any such Passover been observed. But in the eighteenth year of King Josiah, this Passover was celebrated to the Lord in Jerusalem.
>
> Furthermore, Josiah got rid of the mediums and spiritists, the household gods, the idols and all the other detestable things seen in Judah and Jerusalem. This he did to fulfill the requirements of the law written in the book that Hilkiah the priest had discovered in the temple of the Lord. *Neither before nor after Josiah was there a king like him who turned to the Lord as he did—with all his heart and with all his soul and with all his strength*, in accordance with all the Law of Moses. (2 Kings 23:21–25, emphasis added)

We may not remember King Josiah, but God does. There was never a king like him—before him or after him—who turned to the Lord as he did. Do you know what this tells me?

Keep going.

Even when it's hard.

Even when it feels unfair.

Even when you are cleaning up someone else's mess.

Serve with all your heart, with all your soul, and with all your strength. Why? God sees you.

TWELVE

Don't Stay Silent

As we start to talk about Huldah and the role she played in Josiah's story, you may have the same question I had: What was the Book of the Law?

Great question. Let me explain. The people of Israel followed the Torah, which was the book of the law of Moses. It was originally written as one long book but later was divided into five sections: Genesis, Exodus, Leviticus, Numbers, and Deuteronomy.

The "Book of the Law" can refer to the entire book or to a portion. Most scholars agree that the book that was found during the temple repairs was actually Deuteronomy. Or at least a part of it. When this was read to King Josiah, it was the first time he had heard it. It had been available to the previous kings but somehow was lost, most likely during the reign of King Manasseh, who was in rebellion against God.

While this may sound odd to us as modern readers, it actually was quite common for royal documents to be stored within the walls of ancient structures. This was a way to keep them safe and protected for future generations. What was heartbreaking for King Josiah was that the *knowledge* of the Book of the Law had been forgotten.

I want to pause here for a moment. King Manasseh was the grandfather of King Josiah, and he ruled for fifty-five years. His father was King Amon, who ruled for only two years (see 2 Kings 21). That means it took, at the most, only fifty-seven years for the people of Israel to lose the knowledge of the law. Does that sound significant to you?

Right now we live in a cultural climate in the US that in many ways is far from the Christian values this country was founded on. If we think about it, we are in the fifth generation of the "unchurched." That means five generations have gone by since America was considered "churched."[1] For King Josiah, only one generation had passed. In all actuality, we can expect what is happening in our cultural climate. This gives me great encouragement.

You may think I misspoke with that statement. How is any of this encouraging?

Because in the story of King Josiah, and as we will see with Huldah, God raised up leaders who made a difference. King Josiah was remembered as faithful to the Lord—more faithful than any king before or after him. While King Josiah got a late start because the Book of the Law had been lost, he made up for it by working with all his heart, soul, and strength. God saw King Josiah, and He sees us too.

I believe God is raising up leaders who will know Him and make Him known. Leaders who will go outside the four walls of the church to bring the hope of the gospel, real hope, to a world that is broken and hurting.

And, friend, He wants you to be part of this work. I think that is why you are reading this book right now. Because God has more for you than where you have been. He has more for you than what you've been handed. Will it be easy? No. But will He be with you? Absolutely.

Now, let's meet Huldah.

At this point, King Josiah needs to verify whether the Book of the Law that has been found is authentic. To do this, he sends his priest, his scribe, and some of his attendants to the home of a prophet.

> Hilkiah the priest, Ahikam, Akbor, Shaphan and Asaiah went to speak to the prophet Huldah, who was the wife of Shallum son of Tikvah, the son of Harhas, keeper of the wardrobe. She lived in Jerusalem, in the New Quarter. (2 Kings 22:14)

Did you catch that? The *wife* of Shallum. *She* lived in Jerusalem. The prophet of the king is a woman, Huldah. Despite what you may think, it is well known that kings in the ancient Near East had female prophets, or prophetesses as they were called. What I find so interesting about this is that the kings selected who they wanted their royal advisors to be . . . including the prophets. When King Josiah sends the book to Huldah to be verified, it's not like there weren't any other options. In fact, the prophet Jeremiah was also around at the time. (Remember

God is raising up leaders who will know Him and make Him known.

him? He has a whole book in the Bible.) But instead of sending the book to Jeremiah, King Josiah sends it to Huldah. This gives her credibility. She is someone he trusts. Someone he knows can verify the book's authenticity.

At no point does King Josiah, his aides, or even the text make any sort of comment about Huldah being female. The Bible just calls her a prophet. This is a clue to us that at the time her role was not out of the ordinary. The priest, scribe, and aides do not object to Huldah. Instead, they go to her willingly.

The priest and the scribe have spiritual authority, but they are unable to verify the book's authenticity. Priests and scribes had to go through specialized training, and even then only the best ones were selected to serve the king. But prophets? They were appointed based on their relationship with God. This shows us that Huldah possessed a spiritual authority within her circle of influence even though she was a woman. The men in her life sought her out for spiritual wisdom.

That's powerful.

Huldah was sought out because she was known to be able to consult Yahweh directly. She had a relationship with God that was unique. She had been given a spiritual gift that was valuable and needed in her culture.

Friend, do you get it? God *wants* to use women. He *wants* to equip us to serve in a way that is a blessing to those around us. The body of Christ needs your voice, just as the people of Israel needed Huldah's voice. When we surrender our hearts, our gifts, our lives to the Lord, He can use us in some pretty powerful ways.

Huldah is the first person in Scripture to authorize part of the canon. That is significant and something we can't forget in the moments when we feel insecure. Huldah's word validated the Book of the Law as authentic, which prompted Josiah to act.

What if she had stayed silent? What will happen, or won't happen, if *we* stay silent?

It's time to put away the imposter syndrome that plagues most of us, making us think we need a master's degree before God can use us. God will equip us to do what it is that He calls us to do. The only prerequisite? A heart that is surrendered to Him. It is in that place of surrender that we can hear His voice, loud and clear.

We have to recognize that when we are speaking for God, there is an impact to our words. An eternal impact.

THIRTEEN

Speaking the Truth

Huldah's brief storyline in Scripture teaches us so much about what it means to walk out the gift of prophecy. Sometimes we have to look at not just what the stories say but also what they *don't* say. So often with Scripture we have to read between the lines, meditating on the truth of God's Word. In Huldah's case, it is evident that she had a reputation for being a truth teller. Otherwise, she wouldn't have been sought after by the king in a moment when he was desperate for the truth. In a culture where telling little white lies is not just accepted but expected, it's important to be a truth teller.

But I won't sugarcoat things—it is hard to tell the truth, for many reasons. Being willing to say the hard things, to tell the truth when everyone else is silent, is difficult. And the act of actually telling the truth can be a challenge too, especially in a world that tries to say that exaggeration and deception don't count as sins.

For many people who have a prophetic gift, there is a natural element of their personality that seems to be the birthing place for such a gift. However, it can also be a birthing place for sin.

I'm talking about the mouth.

Ever since I was little, I have always been a talker. In first grade, my desk was literally moved into the hall because my teacher couldn't control my temptation to talk. I sat at a desk out in the hall across from the door. I could hear the teacher, but I couldn't talk to anyone. Truth be told, I still talk a lot. I just found a way to turn it into a job.

As I look back on my life, I see so many times when my mouth got me into trouble—with teachers, with bosses, with friends . . . It's my biggest downfall. Sometimes the problem is not that I talk too much. Sometimes it's the words that come out.

I grew up in a family that lied. About everything. Even things that didn't matter.

The juice was red (when it was really orange).

We went to Kmart (when it was really Value City).

We ate chicken (when it was really burgers).

I don't know why this was; it just was. It was like we were allergic to telling the truth. When you are raised in an environment like that, you don't realize lying isn't normal until you are no longer in that environment. Even after I came to Christ at age fifteen, I would often catch myself being dishonest about something. Even at eighteen, I still struggled with this.

I remember getting a brand-new hunter green truck, one that I picked out. It even had air-conditioning and a fancy cassette player (it was the '90s). I got my senior pictures taken next to that truck. I loved it *so* much. But when it came time to tell my friends about it, I told them it was purple. What the heck? Why would I do that? Either they were going to see it, or I was never going to be able to drive it. What was wrong with me? No one would care about the color of my truck. I didn't even like purple. It was like I had no control over what was coming out of my mouth. I had fallen prey to what I had seen displayed by multiple generations in my family without even realizing it.

Alcoholism, gambling, pornography, and every other addictive behavior you can imagine were a part of my family. While I didn't fall into all those sin patterns, I did come away with an addictive personality with a tendency to lie. But as I got out on my own, I knew I didn't want that life. I knew God had something better for me. I knew that if I was going to have any measure of success in my career, in my relationships, in life in general, I needed to get a grip. And so I committed myself to years of therapy. Good mentors. Prayer. Accountability. A God who can change us from the inside out. And thankfully, the Lord delivered me.

The enemy attacks in infancy what he fears in maturity.

Sometimes sin patterns are repeated throughout generations because they are taught through behavior and exposure. But there is good news. We have a God who is in the business of breaking what the Bible calls generational curses. This God can redeem and restore *all* things. Even the things the enemy meant to use for destruction in our lives.

I am pretty confident I know the reason my mouth was such a struggle for me when I was younger. Want to know what it is? The enemy attacks in infancy what he fears in maturity.

Let me say that again. The enemy attacks in infancy what he fears in maturity.

Years later, through God's redemptive work in my life, I have a podcast (two, actually) through which I teach people about Jesus. (Using my words.)

I have written multiple books about Jesus. (Using my words.)

I have opportunities to speak to audiences about Jesus. (Using my words.)

I have the amazing privilege of traveling to different countries to tell people about a God who loves them and has a plan for their lives. (Using my words.)

God had a plan for my words as He redeemed not only my words but also my heart.

The enemy attacked in infancy what he feared in maturity.

I wonder if that's the same for you. I wonder if you have ever struggled with what comes out of your mouth. Maybe for you the problem is not the words you say as much as the tone of your voice. A negative tone can be learned. Or it can be the default when we are stressed, depressed, or anxious.

As believers, we are called to speak life, and so this is an area of our lives where we *have* to get a grip. Our future testimony depends on it. If there is a call of God on your life to know Him and to make Him known, then you *have* to be seen as a person of integrity. Someone who speaks the truth in love. It's not just about the *truth* part. It's also about the *love* part.

Telling the truth can be hard for a different reason. Sometimes it's hard to speak the truth when we know the truth will hurt someone. Part of the calling of a prophet is to speak the truth in all situations, even when the news may not be what someone wants to hear. If the Lord has given us wisdom, discernment, or insight into a situation, and it's bad news, we still have a responsibility to speak. Even if we know it's not going to be received well. Sometimes we need to speak the truth in love even if we are the ones it's going to hurt. What do I mean? Well, not everyone is ready to handle the truth.

Not too long ago, I felt the Lord prompting me to speak up about a situation that was grieving His heart. It concerned someone in a leadership role, and I knew the conversation was going to be difficult. While I tried to temper my words with a reminder about God's mercy and forgiveness, it quickly became clear that the person was prepared to shoot the messenger.

Was I speaking the truth? Yes. In love? Also, yes. Did they receive it? Nope.

And if I am honest, it burdened my heart for weeks. This person knew I had a prophetic gifting. They knew I cared about them and the people they were leading. And still, they rejected what I had to say in a way that felt so heavy.

After I spent some time praying about this, the Lord spoke something into my heart that at the time I sensed was just for me. But now as I write this, I think it may be for you too. I will share it here:

I see your heart.

Sometimes speaking the truth is like turning on the light in a room that has been dark for a very long time. Your life is filled with My light, and it's natural that you want to take the light into the darkness, because that's what I've called you to do.

Not everyone is ready for the light. When someone has been living in the darkness, it's like they have been living in a very dark room. When someone flips on the light, it's painful. For some, it's the first time they have ever had the light on, and their eyes hurt. Their first instinct is to shut their eyes tightly, to try to shut out the light.

For some, eventually, the light will reveal what has been hidden in the darkness, and they will be thankful for the light. But not everyone is ready for the light; they prefer the darkness. When the darkness becomes too dark, they will welcome the pain of the light.

Be a light bringer, even if those who are in darkness are not ready for the pain of the light.

Rachael, your name means "lamb." You hear the voice of your Shepherd.

Before you were in your mother's womb, I knew you.

I know you still.

I set you apart for this.

To be a light bringer.

Shine brightly, dear one.

Always wanting to measure a word *from* God against the Word *of* God, I immediately went to the Bible and found some amazing confirmations that blessed me so much. Here are a few of them:

> When Jesus spoke again to the people, he said, "I am the light of the world. Whoever follows me will never walk in darkness, but will have the light of life." (John 8:12)

> Then Jesus told them, "You are going to have the light just a little while longer. Walk while you have the light, before darkness

overtakes you. Whoever walks in the dark does not know where they are going. Believe in the light while you have the light, so that you may become children of light." (John 12:35–36)

The unfolding of your words gives light;
    it gives understanding to the simple. (Ps. 119:130)

But you are a chosen people, a royal priesthood, a holy nation, God's special possession, that you may declare the praises of him who called you out of darkness into his wonderful light. (1 Pet. 2:9)

This is the message we have heard from him and declare to you: God is light; in him there is no darkness at all. If we claim to have fellowship with him and yet walk in the darkness, we lie and do not live out the truth. But if we walk in the light, as he is in the light, we have fellowship with one another, and the blood of Jesus, his Son, purifies us from all sin.

If we claim to be without sin, we deceive ourselves and the truth is not in us. If we confess our sins, he is faithful and just and will forgive us our sins and purify us from all unrighteousness. (1 John 1:5–9)

The light shines in the darkness, and the darkness has not overcome it. (John 1:5)

Your word is a lamp for my feet,
    a light on my path. (Ps. 119:105)

Do not gloat over me, my enemy!
    Though I have fallen, I will rise.

> Though I sit in darkness,
> the LORD will be my light. (Mic. 7:8)

While I am in the world, I am the light of the world. (John 9:5)

You are the light of the world. A town built on a hill cannot be hidden. Neither do people light a lamp and put it under a bowl. Instead they put it on its stand, and it gives light to everyone in the house. In the same way, let your light shine before others, that they may see your good deeds and glorify your Father in heaven. (Matt. 5:14–16)

Friend, keep speaking the truth even when it's hard. You are a light bringer.

FOURTEEN

This Doesn't Look Right

Huldah was a woman who spoke the truth, and her reputation for being able to speak directly with Yahweh was the very thing that qualified her for the job King Josiah had for her. He wanted to know what she had to say about the book that had been found, even if he didn't like the answer.

> She said to them, "This is what the Lord, the God of Israel, says: Tell the man who sent you to me, 'This is what the Lord says: I am going to bring disaster on this place and its people, according to everything written in the book the king of Judah has read. Because they have forsaken me and burned incense to other gods and aroused my anger by all the idols their hands have made, my anger will burn against this place and will not be quenched.' Tell the king of Judah, who sent you to inquire of the Lord, 'This is what the Lord, the God of Israel, says concerning the words you heard: Because your heart was responsive and you humbled yourself before the Lord when you heard what I have spoken against this place

and its people—that they would become a curse and be laid waste—and because you tore your robes and wept in my presence, I also have heard you, declares the LORD. Therefore I will gather you to your ancestors, and you will be buried in peace. Your eyes will not see all the disaster I am going to bring on this place.'"

So they took her answer back to the king. (2 Kings 22:15–20)

Huldah confirmed that the book was real. But that wasn't all. She also warned that the Lord was going to bring disaster to Jerusalem because of the disobedience of the Hebrew people. They were following the false gods of other nations. They had completely forgotten about Yahweh, the one who had rescued them out of the hands of the Egyptians and given them the promised land. They had made idols and worshiped them. They lived a life of sin that extinguished their need for God.

It was a pretty dark time in Israel's history. But there is something we need to remember.

God saw Josiah. Scripture says that because Josiah's heart was responsive, he humbled himself before the Lord, and he grieved when he learned the truth. God heard him. He saw his tears, saw his humility, and saw his heart. As a result, the promise of God for Josiah was peace. Peace that would keep Josiah from seeing the disaster that was the judgment for those who refused to yield to Yahweh. Death would spare him from seeing the destruction.

But the destruction was still coming.

I don't know about you, but I may have been tempted to just give up. But that's not what Josiah did. Instead, he did the opposite. He worked harder. He not only restored the temple but also reformed and restored the covenant between God and His chosen people.

When I think about that, my first question is, Why? Why would Josiah continue the work when he knew what was coming? Well, the answer is actually pretty simple.

He was faithful. He wasn't faithful because of what it could get him. He wasn't faithful because of what others thought. He wasn't even faithful because of his family. He was faithful because of who God was in his life.

There will be times in your life when you feel like you are working for nothing. Like there is too much work to do, too much need. There will be times when others will tell you that your work is in vain and that you live in a world that will never appreciate the work you do.

Keep working anyway. God sees you. He sees your heart. The promise of peace that comes from a life lived faithfully is worth the effort of staying the course.

Scripture makes it clear that there was no king like Josiah before him or after him. The reason for that is because of the way he faithfully served God even when everything around him was falling apart.

I feel that. Sometimes I take a look around this fallen world we live in. With wars, and famine, and poverty . . . it can feel overwhelming. But the call to be faithful to God has more to do with Him and less to do with me. Or the world around me.

So stay the course. Keep going when it's hard. Keep your eyes on the One who gives peace amid chaos.

A dear friend of mine passed away a couple years ago. She loved the Lord. She served Him with everything in her heart.

She was faithful to the very end. Yet she still died, far too young. Many in our community questioned how God could take such a beautiful woman, knowing how faithfully she served Him. Maybe you have had something similar happen in your life and have similar questions.

Why didn't God heal her? My answer to that is that He did. He just didn't heal her until she reached the other side of heaven.

The reality is that sometimes we won't see the fruit of our labor this side of heaven. Sometimes we will give a prophetic word to someone, and it won't make sense to them for twenty years. Sometimes we won't ever get confirmation that what we said or did resonated with them.

It's okay. Remain faithful anyway.

King Josiah could not turn things around for Israel in his lifetime, but God still protected and honored his sacrifice and work. God saw him.

He sees you too.

In the end, it may seem like Huldah got it wrong. The death of Josiah was anything but peaceful. He died on the battlefield.

> While Josiah was king, Pharaoh Necho king of Egypt went up to the Euphrates River to help the king of Assyria. King Josiah marched out to meet him in battle, but Necho faced him and killed him at Megiddo. Josiah's servants brought his body in a chariot from Megiddo to Jerusalem and buried him in his own tomb. And the people of the land took Jehoahaz son of Josiah and anointed him and made him king in place of his father. (2 Kings 23:29–30)

Josiah's life likely didn't end the way he thought it would. Yet he died before he could see the destruction of his people and before they fell into the hands of the Babylonians. So even though his actual death wasn't peaceful, he did die in peace before seeing the suffering of his people.

Huldah was right; her prophecy just didn't look the way he thought it would.

Giving a prophetic word to someone can often feel like that. When God gives us a word, whether it is a specific Scripture passage, a warning, or something else, we have to release that word without expectation. What happens may not be what we expected, and the difference may be difficult for us. But as we surrender even our words to God, we submit our will to His. Ultimately, it's God's will that matters. We reveal His words to His people. How that plays out is for God to decide. Our job? Remain faithful.

FIFTEEN

Public Versus Private

As we study Huldah, we see that there is something different about the way God used her when we compare her to Miriam or Deborah. With the first two, we saw God use their gifts in a corporate, public way. Miriam helped lead the Hebrew people out of Egypt, through the Red Sea, and into the wilderness. Her gifts were used to lead and encourage the corporate body of people. Similarly, Deborah's gifts were used as part of a battle plan that brought a victory that led to peace in Israel for forty years.

With Huldah, even though she was called a prophet, her words were said in private. She was used by God to deliver a word to King Josiah that confirmed what he already suspected to be true. Her words were shared in her home and only with the king's advisors. I think this is important to point out.

Not everything is for everyone.

Sometimes God will give you a word or show you something from Scripture that is meant to impact your circle of influence. It's to encourage, empower, or equip God's people for His work in their lives or community. Other times God will give you a word that is meant just for you and should be held in your heart. And still other times God will give you a word that should be shared only in private. That doesn't mean there isn't an impact.

As we see in Huldah's case, her prophetic words to the king are what prompt him to make significant changes and empower him to do the work God calls him to do. Her words are the catalyst for significant reform within the religious context of the time. She is able to speak into the situation because she is trusted by the king. To possess the status and reputation she had and not be questioned by the king's advisors, she had to have spoken the words of God prior to this situation in a way that proved her ability to interact and speak directly with the Lord. The king knew this, and perhaps Huldah had even spoken these kinds of words to the king himself before this in private.

The point is we have to know what to do with the words God gives us. When God shows us something from His Word, we need to be open to what *He* wants us to do with it. There can be a danger in wanting to share everything with everyone. It is an amazing thing to get to a place of confidence in our relationship with the Lord. But as we learned with Miriam, confidence can quickly become a trap. We must remain humble and surrender even the words God gives us to His will and design. How do we navigate this? There are a couple things to keep in mind.

First, we need to make sure that we are truly hearing the voice of God. Are we hearing God's voice? Our voice? Or the voice of the enemy? How do we tell? For starters, God's voice will never contradict God's Word. I know I keep saying this, but it really is the first litmus test. I repeat it because I want you to remember it. God's voice will never contradict God's Word.

God's voice will never contradict God's Word.

Assuming you have already verified the word God has given you with Scripture, the second test is to see if it is something that came from you.

Ultimately, the way we discern the voice of God is by knowing Him. How do we know Him? By spending time with Him. Again, this may sound like I am repeating myself because I am. There are no shortcuts here. We cannot skip over the relationship part to get to the spiritual gifts part. Spiritual gifts flow out of our relationship with Him. Have you been spending time with Him? Have you been in the Word? Spending time in worship? What about prayer? As we study Him and His Word, we will find it easier to recognize His voice when He speaks to us. It is really hard to distinguish God's voice from our own voice if we haven't been spending any time with Him.

Then it's time to pray about what God wants us to do with the message He has given. Is it just for us? Is it for others we are in relationship with? Is it a private word for someone? Let's assume that if the God of the universe, the Creator of heaven and earth, is going to speak a word to us, we can trust Him to show us what to do with that word.

I understand that sometimes this isn't easy. It can be really hard to sit with something and just pray about what to do with it. When I was younger, I would just blurt out whatever I heard, thinking that it must be for whoever was in the room. As I have matured in this area, God has shown me that the best way is *His* way—which means waiting on His timing. Sometimes that means holding something in my heart for way longer than I want to. If that is too difficult, I will write it down.

Recently, I was invited to an event where I didn't know a single person in the room. It was a small, intimate setting that was focused on worship. I wasn't there to serve, to speak, or to "perform" at all. Simply just to be in the presence of Jesus. However, during worship, the Lord started to show me things about three people in the room. I was with people from many denominational backgrounds, and I didn't want to offend anyone. But still, there was a pressing in my spirit. So I did what I often do these days. I wrote down what I heard. Then I prayed a quick prayer, asking the Lord to show me what to do. I went back to worshiping and, in all honesty, forgot about the people for the rest of the morning.

Later that day, after lunch, some rest, and time in fellowship, we gathered together again for afternoon worship. Our host started by checking in with us as a group, asking if the Lord had done anything in our hearts during the day. The first person the Lord had given me a word for stood up and shared that the Lord was starting a deep work in his heart. He had been struggling with some things in his personal life, and he was grateful for the time that day just to be with Jesus. The leader of the group decided to pray for him at that moment, and as we started to pray, the Lord interrupted my thoughts.

Now.

Really? Okay.

As the prayer finished, I asked for permission to share what the Lord had shown me earlier that day. He gave me permission, and I proceeded to read to him what I had written during the morning session. With tears in his eyes, he thanked me. I won't share what I said, but he later told me that it was so specific, even down to what happened to him that very day, that it was confirmation to him that the Lord saw him. My words encouraged him in the way he needed, in the moment he needed it.

After he sat down, a woman started speaking from the back of the room, sharing some pain about things in her life and what the Lord had done in her downtime that day. And don't you know it, she was one of the three the Lord had given me words for that morning. We prayed for her, and as we were finishing, I heard it again.

Now.

Okay. Not questioning it this time, I asked her permission to share. She nodded, and I poured out to her the words of love and encouragement the Lord had given me for her earlier that day. With tears, she received the love He was offering to her in that moment in a very tangible way.

At this point, I was not surprised one bit to see who spoke up next. Who else but the third person the Lord had given me a word for that morning? As he shared, the words that came out of his mouth were some of the very same words I had written down. We prayed over him, and again, after asking permission, I read every single word on that page. By this time, we were all chuckling a little bit because of how God works.

Could I have just blurted out what God had showed me that morning, in the moment, right then and there? Of course.

But surrendering the words and the timing of the messages ministered not just to those individuals but to all of us in the room—including me.

God's timing is not our timing, and His ways are not our ways.

And for that, I am so thankful.

SIXTEEN

How to Be Like Huldah

In this study of Huldah, I hope you have been able to glean the lessons we can learn from her influence as you strive to live a life that is surrendered to the Lord. I drew insights about Huldah from 2 Kings 22. But an almost identical account of her story is found in 2 Chronicles 34. The Chronicles of the kings were written during the time of the kings to help document what was happening historically. The Chronicles were the final part of the Hebrew Bible, for a reason. In our Bibles, the Chronicles are two distinct books, but originally they were written as one larger book. The reason for this is because of their length, and how difficult it was to use only one scroll for the entire thing. Using two scrolls made it easier to use and reference. In our Bibles today, Chronicles follows the books of Samuel and Kings. Much of Chronicles uses information from those books, so reading Chronicles can seem repetitive. But originally the book of Chronicles was used as a summary of the Hebrew Bible, starting with Adam and ending with Israel's return from exile.

Why is this important?

Well, I think it's significant that the chronicler included Huldah's portion in Josiah's story. King Josiah was an example of faithfulness to God and was remembered in the Chronicles as a good leader.

A good leader who sought the counsel of a woman.

I have to believe that a good leader, one called the *most* faithful king of Israel, would not consult a woman if it was not part of God's plan for good leadership. I have to believe that a good leader who then enacted religious reform based on that woman's words would not be remembered for that religious reform if she was out of line with her words. While Huldah's actual words in Scripture cover only five verses (ten if we count them twice because of Chronicles), we can learn so much from the context of her story. Huldah spoke the truth, even when it was hard. Speak the truth, friend. Say the hard things. Say them with love, but don't stay silent. The world needs your voice.

Sometimes it may be easy for us to forget that our voice, and using it to point people back to Jesus, is a spiritual gift. However, we don't have to feel pressure about what it means to use our voices for Him. We have to remember that even when we are talking about our voice being used by God, our spiritual gifts are exactly that, gifts.

While there is always some element of being a good steward with the gifts God has given us, this is different from honing a skill. Spiritual gifts are gifts from God. We have access to them through the Holy Spirit. But the burden isn't on us to perform. God is the one who decides when and if He wants us to speak up or minister in this way. Our job is to place our heart in a posture so it is ready to receive. The rest is up to Him. I think it gives us some freedom to realize that there isn't something wrong with us if we don't hear from Him. There are times I feel like I "should" have a word for someone, and I don't. But that's not the way God works. Sometimes God works in a way that we least expect it, when we are with people we don't know and are just trying to get to the bathroom. Sometimes God doesn't follow the strategic ministry plan we have laid out for Him. Sometimes He just wants us to love His kids and help them feel seen and heard.

If you want to grow in this area, here are a couple things that have been so helpful for me to remember as I have learned how to allow God to use me in this gift:

1. Let the outcome be His.

As with so many other areas in our spiritual lives, obedience is our part to play when God gives us a word. Obedience to remain silent, obedience to pray, obedience to speak up. Whatever God is telling us to do, our primary concern is our obedience to Him. He is the one who will use the word in the way He sees fit. Sometimes this means taking a risk and feeling like we got it wrong. There have been times in my life when I took the risk and spoke to someone as God burdened my heart with a message for them. In the moment, the enemy convinced me I was crazy or that the person thought I was crazy. But often, sometimes even years later, that person came back to me to share what the Lord did in their lives through that message. I think in many ways our obedience in that moment acts like a radio dial. Older radios have a dial that you must turn to change channels. The closer you get to the channel, the clearer the voice becomes. The farther away from the channel, the fuzzier it becomes. Obedience is like the dial. When we obey God in what He is telling us to do, it is easier to hear His voice the next time. Obedience helps us "tune in" to what He is trying to say to us.

2. Never stop seeking the gifts.

Spiritual growth is slow. So, so slow. Yet besides coming to Jesus in the first place, it's the most important thing we will do this side of heaven. As we continue to grow in our relationship with the Lord, it's important that we don't stop seeking the gifts, all the gifts. Scripture makes this clear. So many people earnestly seek the gift of speaking in tongues, yet Scripture says that prophecy is the superior gift.

> Pursue love, yet earnestly desire spiritual gifts, but especially that you may prophesy. For the one who speaks in a tongue does not speak to people, but to God; for no one understands, but in his spirit he speaks mysteries. But the one who prophesies speaks to people for edification, exhortation, and consolation. The one who speaks in a tongue edifies himself; but the one who prophesies edifies the church. Now I wish that you all spoke in tongues, but rather that you would prophesy; and greater is the one who prophesies than the one who speaks in tongues, unless he interprets, so that the church may receive edification. (1 Cor. 14:1–5 NASB)

Are we truly seeking spiritual gifts in our lives?

Pursue love. Check.

Desire spiritual gifts. Check.

But prophesy? Um . . . are you sure?

Scripture says that prophecies edify, exhort, and console the body of Christ. What do those words mean exactly? I'm glad you asked.

Edify, *oikodomē*: "the act of building up, the act of one who promotes another's growth in Christian wisdom, piety, happiness, and holiness."[1] This word is actually used to describe architecture, the literal buildings of the temple complex, in Matthew 24:1. Prophecy literally builds faith for other people.

Exhort, *paraklēsis*: "encouragement, refreshment."[2] This word is used to describe the comfort of the Holy Spirit.

Console, *paramythia*: "calming and consoling, with the purpose of persuading."[3] This word appears only once in the entire New Testament. This word is about calming and comforting in a way that convinces people that God is real and that He sees them.

Prophecy is a powerful spiritual gift that God uses in a unique way to draw people to Himself. And yet it's one of the gifts we so often shy away from. Fear is a tool the enemy uses to keep God's people bound in their insecurity, in their sin.

No more. It's time for the body of Christ to start building each other up the way God intended. Never stop seeking the gifts. Especially prophecy. What does prophecy mean?

Prophesy, *prophēteuō*: "to speak forth by divine inspiration."[4]

There are times when each one of us can hear the voice of God and can speak up on His behalf. And when that happens, we can have the confidence to know that it is God speaking through us.

QUESTIONS TO PONDER

- What steps can you take to rid your life of any "idols" or distractions that may be hindering your relationship with God? What might those things be in your life?
- Have you ever felt called to undo or address issues from your past or your family's past? How have you approached this? While we recognize we are not to blame for the past mistakes of our families, we can also change the faith legacy we are leaving behind for future generations.
- How do you balance the need for immediate action with the understanding that some restoration work takes time and effort? Reflect on the fact that we are called to work toward a goal that may not be realized this side of heaven.
- Have you experienced a time when you discovered something new in God's Word that changed your perspective or actions? How did you respond? Plan to share that with others the next time it happens.
- What does it mean to you to be a "light bringer" in your community? How can you shine God's light in dark places even when it's challenging? Who is someone you can bring some light to right now? Pray for them this very moment.

Spend some time in prayer, preparing your heart for the next time God asks you to speak the truth, especially if it is difficult. Pray for wisdom to know when you should speak up and when you should remain silent.

And never stop seeking the gifts of God.

KNOWING GOD'S VOICE IN REAL LIFE

Healing

It started out as any normal worship service. I was looking forward to getting filled up spiritually as I focused my heart and mind on the Lord. As I was praising God for His goodness, He showed me the image of a neck. It was the back of a neck, and it looked like my hands were touching either side.

My neck was fine, so I assumed this meant I was supposed to pray for someone else. I opened my eyes and looked around the room, but everyone looked fine. I silently prayed for God to show me what He wanted me to do, and I continued worshiping.

Before long, I felt someone sit down next to me. As I opened my eyes, I saw a woman sitting there, eyes closed, lost in worship. I didn't even need to hear God's voice at that moment because I knew in my spirit that she was the one I was supposed to pray for.

"I'm so sorry to bother you, but do you need prayer for your neck?" I asked, already knowing the answer.

She looked at me wide-eyed and nodded.

I placed my hands on either side of her neck, just as the Lord had shown me a few moments earlier. I prayed healing over her, and within a matter of moments, God healed her.

She went on to share with me that on the way there she had gotten into a car accident. She thought she was fine, but as she was sitting there she made the decision to go to the ER afterward because her neck was really starting to hurt.

The Lord knew that even though I had no idea. I am so thankful for the God who sees us, who sees our pain, and who heals.

One thing I have seen over the last few years is that when a person grows in a spiritual gift, additional spiritual gifts come. I never set out to ask God for the gift of healing. Instead, my prayer has always been to be used by Him in whatever capacity He sees fit. Often the healing gift comes along with a word. Sometimes the healing is emotional; sometimes it is physical. I can't control the gift any more than I can control the wind. All I can do is be obedient when it comes.

PART 4

ANNA

SEVENTEEN

Watching in the Waiting

Oppression was nothing new for the Jewish people. For centuries, they waited for the Messiah, God's rescue plan, to come and save them and restore their relationship with God. Prophets in the Old Testament, both male and female, spoke to God's people on God's behalf as they waited on His promise. The period between the Old Testament and the New Testament is often characterized as the "silent years" because those prophetic voices had gone silent. While God was setting the stage for Jesus's arrival, many in Israel had given up on the promised Messiah. Roman oppression was harsh, and many of the Jewish people felt that God's silence was His judgment on the nation for their sin. It is during this time that Jesus arrives on the scene, born to a teenage virgin amid stables and shepherds.

> When the time came for the purification rites required by the Law of Moses, Joseph and Mary took [Jesus] to Jerusalem to

present him to the Lord (as it is written in the Law of the Lord, "Every firstborn male is to be consecrated to the Lord"), and to offer a sacrifice in keeping with what is said in the Law of the Lord: "a pair of doves or two young pigeons."

Now there was a man in Jerusalem called Simeon, who was righteous and devout. He was waiting for the consolation of Israel, and the Holy Spirit was on him. It had been revealed to him by the Holy Spirit that he would not die before he had seen the Lord's Messiah. Moved by the Spirit, he went into the temple courts. When the parents brought in the child Jesus to do for him what the custom of the Law required, Simeon took him in his arms and praised God, saying:

"Sovereign Lord, as you have promised,
  you may now dismiss your servant in peace.
For my eyes have seen your salvation,
  which you have prepared in the sight of all nations:
a light for revelation to the Gentiles,
  and the glory of your people Israel."

The child's father and mother marveled at what was said about him. Then Simeon blessed them and said to Mary, his mother: "This child is destined to cause the falling and rising of many in Israel, and to be a sign that will be spoken against, so that the thoughts of many hearts will be revealed. And a sword will pierce your own soul too." (Luke 2:22–35)

While many had given up on the Messiah, two people clung to His promised coming: Simeon and Anna.

Each time we set out to examine the story of a woman who heard from the Lord as a prophetess in Scripture, we see that she is coupled with a male counterpart. Miriam and Moses.

Deborah and Barak. Huldah and King Josiah. And now Anna and Simeon. Sometimes these relationships contrast each other, and sometimes they work in tandem. Beginning with the creation story with Adam and Eve, we see that God's design is a picture of completion when men and women work together to serve God's kingdom. God created us to serve together, with the understanding that each gender brings unique gifts to the body of Christ. Without each other, we do not experience the fullness God intended. Sometimes people in Scripture got it right, and sometimes they got it wrong. The same is true for us. But over and over, we see a God who uses both genders in powerful ways. So, like with the other women we have studied, it is difficult to study Anna without getting to know Simeon.

To study Simeon, we first consider Mary and Joseph. Jesus has been born in quite a miraculous way, and Mary and Joseph are part of the biggest miracle the world will ever see. God chose them to be the parents of Jesus, and they are taking their roles seriously. Because of this, Mary and Joseph are raising Jesus within the traditional laws of their Jewish heritage. This means they need to head to the temple shortly after His birth. Modern readers may find it difficult to understand why this was such a priority so early in Jesus's life. In biblical times, several things needed to happen in the temple. Because of the process of childbirth, Mary needed to go to the temple for her ritual purification. Likely, Joseph needed purification as well, since he probably helped Mary in the childbirth process and would have become "unclean" as a result. In addition, it was typical within the Jewish culture to present and dedicate the child to the Lord. There was also the issue of circumcision that needed to be addressed in the temple. So Mary and Joseph go to the temple, taking with them two birds for their offering. Two doves were the traditional offering of those that were poor, which is an indication of the humble beginnings Jesus was born into.

As Mary and Joseph faithfully enter the temple, they meet Simeon, who immediately recognizes what is happening. He has been waiting for this exact moment. God had promised him that he would not die until he saw the Messiah. And Simeon is old. He has been waiting a long time. But one of the things I love about Simeon is that he had not grown weary in his waiting. He has been waiting on the promise of God, but he hasn't been passively waiting. He has been actively watching.

Like many of the people of Israel at the time, many of us get tired of waiting, especially when God is silent. We somehow think that God is taking too long. It seems like whatever is supposed to be, it should have happened by now. Years go by and nothing changes. Perhaps things even get worse. Or maybe the people who used to be supportive and waited alongside us have given up and moved on. The enemy convinces us that what we're waiting for is never going to happen and we should give up too.

There have been times in my own life when God's silence felt like a broken promise. Maybe you have been there too.

The healing you are praying for hasn't happened.

The job you are waiting on just doesn't materialize.

The person you are praying for to get saved still has a hardened heart.

The spouse you are waiting to meet hasn't appeared.

I don't know what you are waiting on or what promise of God feels late in coming, but I do know that in the waiting we must keep watching. It's easy to stop watching. We get weary and take our eyes off God. We get distracted by the world or settle for the enemy's version of what God has promised. We settle for something temporary that can never satisfy.

But Simeon? He was watching. He was so faithful in watching that he immediately knew what was happening when Jesus came through that door. He recognized the miracle moment because his eyes were focused on God.

What if we do that too? I have to believe that if we are watching God with the kind of intention and focus that Simeon had, we will start to focus less on the promise and more on the One who made it. Our relationship with God will become more important than the fulfillment of the promise because it teaches us who God is. Keeping our focus on God and watching while waiting develops our character as we come to truly understand the God who keeps His promises.

If we are watching God with the kind of intention and focus that Simeon had, we will start to focus less on the promise and more on the One who made it.

Simeon, while wise and obedient, was just a man. But Scripture gives him two important characteristics:

> And there was a man in Jerusalem whose name was Simeon; and this man was righteous and devout, looking forward to

> the consolation of Israel; and the Holy Spirit was upon him. (Luke 2:25 NASB)

What does that mean? Well, to better understand this verse, let's break it down word by word in the original Greek.

Righteous, *dikaios*: "upright, virtuous, keeping the commands of God."

Devout, *eulabēs*: "taking hold well, reverencing God."

Looking forward, *prosdechomai*: "to expect the fulfillment of promises."

Consolation, *paraklēsis*: "comfort."[1]

The "consolation of Israel" means the salvation and peace that will come with the Messiah through forgiveness and restoration.

So Simeon was a man who kept the commands of God, took hold of the promise, and expected God to fulfill His promise to comfort and save Israel through the birth of the Messiah. Simeon was actively watching for the fulfillment of the promise of God in his life.

Let me ask you something. Do you do that? I don't know that I always do. In theory, I do. But in actuality, waiting is hard. We are impatient people who have trained ourselves to want things instantly. Yet we see Simeon watching in the waiting. For years. And years. And *years*.

Watching in the waiting.

What happens next is nothing short of miraculous. Simeon immediately recognizes who Jesus is. And what is his response? He praises God. He praises Him for the fulfillment of the promise, and he declares Jesus the Savior of the world.

Let's think about that for a moment. Simeon kept his eyes on God. He didn't give up because the promise took too long or the silence was too loud. The result? He was able to declare the promise of God not just in his own life but in the lives of those around him.

That's powerful, friend. Think of everything we could be missing out on because we give up too soon. We could be abandoning the very thing God created us for. For Simeon, that thing was the moment he met Jesus. That moment changed everything for him. He finally had peace seeing God's promise fulfilled. His relationship with God gave him purpose and that purpose was what defined him.

It would be easy to think this was the end. That everything ended in a happily ever after. But we know that isn't the case. We know that this is just the beginning of a long journey Jesus will take, eventually leading Him to the cross. What Simeon knew, what he shared with Mary and Joseph, is something we have to realize as believers. The promise is not always without pain.

Simeon warns that people will react to Jesus the same way they react to God. He will cause division, and people will have to decide what they believe about Him. Praising Jesus and serving God don't mean that life will be easy. In fact, the opposite is often true. Ministry often produces rejection. Simeon speaks a truth to Mary that many of us know: Mothers experience pain when their children do. Simeon's foreshadowing is meant to prepare Mary for what's to come. The gospel is offensive to those who are living in sin.

Friend, we can't forget that Jesus has the victory. Simeon watched in the waiting because he knew it would be true.

But we know something incredible that even Simeon did not: We know the end of the story. We know what happened after three days. We know the peace and presence of the Holy Spirit. Simeon didn't know all that.

So why did he hold on so long? Well, the Holy Spirit gave him the promise in the first place. There is a confidence that comes when we *know* that God has spoken something into our lives. That confidence is not the same as the confidence the world offers. It's something that gets embedded into our spirits in a way that it becomes part of us. Confidence in our relationship with God is the very thing that will help us hold on when the waiting feels too long.

It's what helps us to keep watching in the waiting.

EIGHTEEN

Worship in the Waiting

Simeon wasn't the only one waiting on the promised Messiah. While Simeon was watching in the waiting, Anna was worshiping in the waiting. In fact, Anna's story begins and ends with worship.

> There was also a prophet, Anna, the daughter of Penuel, of the tribe of Asher. She was very old; she had lived with her husband seven years after her marriage, and then was a widow until she was eighty-four. She never left the temple but worshiped night and day, fasting and praying. Coming up to them at that very moment, she gave thanks to God and spoke about the child to all who were looking forward to the redemption of Jerusalem.
>
> When Joseph and Mary had done everything required by the Law of the Lord, they returned to Galilee to their own town of Nazareth. And the child grew and became strong; he was filled with wisdom, and the grace of God was on him. (Luke 2:36–40)

Even though Anna's story is summed up in just a handful of verses, that does not mean it isn't significant. Anna is the only woman called a prophet in the New Testament. While other women operate within the spiritual gift of prophecy, she is the only one with the designation of prophet. Like some of the other women we have been learning about, Anna was also a worshiper. Scripture says she worshiped night and day in the temple in Jerusalem. I don't want to skip too quickly past that part, because I think it's significant.

Anna was elderly at the time of Jesus's birth. We learn in this short passage that she was married for only seven years before her husband passed away and then remained a widow until she was eighty-four years old.

Anna was used to waiting. I sometimes wonder if I will ever get used to waiting; it's one of my least favorite things. But Anna, whose name means "grace,"[1] waited patiently on the Lord for a very long time. I think sometimes we forget to stop and think about what life was like for different people in the Bible. We read their stories and jump right to the good part without thinking about how they actually got there.

Anna was acquainted with suffering. Widows at this time were some of the most marginalized people in society. They typically were unable to own property, which almost always sentenced them to a life of poverty. They led lonely lives and largely depended on strangers just to survive. I have spent a lot of time with people living in poverty, and I have seen firsthand the suffering that can accompany those who have little ability to provide for themselves.

I think about times in my life when I allowed difficult circumstances to drive me away from Jesus. Perhaps you have been there too. The pain of grief and loss can be so overwhelming at times that it consumes us. But not Anna. Instead, it propelled her into a life of service, and the temple became her dwelling place.

Think about that for a minute with me. Amid the pain of her circumstances, Anna found her dwelling place in the Lord. What a powerful example for those of us who have been there. The enemy would want us to believe that grief and pain are good enough excuses to leave our relationship with God behind. Yet God's plan is to draw us close. The way we heal from those kinds of experiences is by allowing the Lord into the pain of our circumstances. He longs to be present with us in our pain so that He can heal it. But so many times we either try to ignore that it's there in the first place or try to hide it from Him because it feels too dark.

Friend, the darkness is never too dark for the One who made the light.

You may not be going through grief like Anna was, but you may encounter seasons in your life that are painful. Or characterized by waiting . . . loooooong periods of waiting. In those moments, God longs to be present with you. Remember Anna in those moments when you are tempted to run away and, instead, lean into the kind of healing that can come only through abiding in Him.

The darkness is never too dark for the One who made the light.

Another aspect of Anna's life that we learn about is that she is the daughter of Penuel, who is from the tribe of Asher. What you may not realize is that this fact alone tells us something about her spiritual heritage. As

Figure 18.1 **Tribes of Israel**

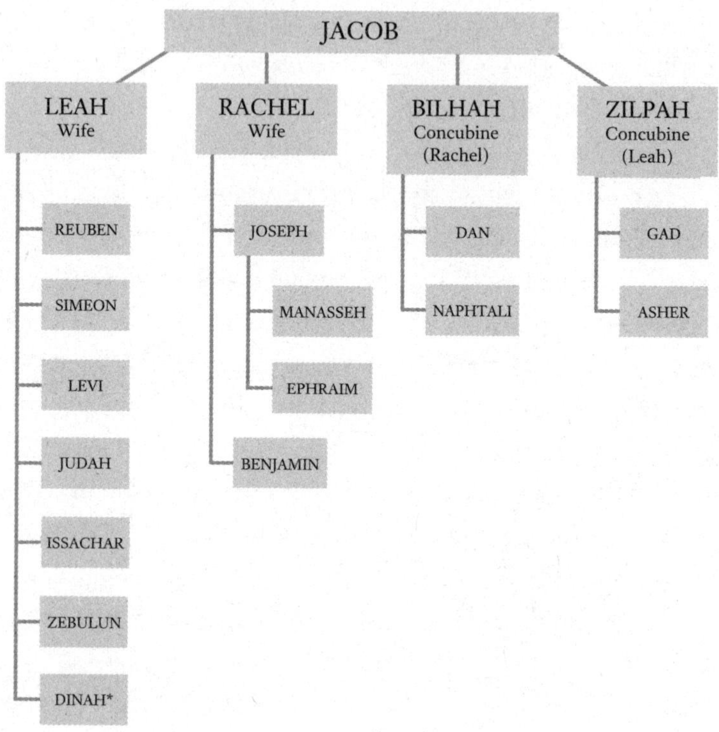

*did not become a tribe of Israel

you may remember, Jacob's descendants eventually became the twelve tribes of Israel (see fig. 18.1). After the kingdom of Israel split in two, Asher was one of the ten tribes of Israel that were in the northern kingdom, and that's what I want to focus on here.

The tribes of the northern kingdom were scattered throughout the Assyrian Empire after Israel was conquered in 722 BC. Many of these Israelites lost their heritage as they assimilated into foreign cultures, adopting other gods and abandoning their relationship with Yahweh. But some of them, apparently Anna's family members, remained faithful to God. This tells us so much about the legacy of faith that was handed down to Anna.

Anna is part of the faithful remnant of God's people who remained committed to Yahweh despite their captivity. Anna is the only person mentioned in Scripture to be from the tribe of Asher. We don't learn about her parents or even her husband. But we see their impact and influence in her life as she remains faithful long into her old age.

When we meet Anna, Luke refers to her as a prophet even before she interacts with Jesus and His family. It is not her interaction with them that makes her into a prophet. Instead, she is already known to be a prophet. This means that she regularly speaks God's heart to God's people on God's behalf.

Anna did not allow her circumstances—grief, poverty, pain—to separate her from the work of God in her life. Instead, she adopted a lifestyle of worship. She became an attendant of the temple, remaining faithful to God as she worshiped day and night. And we see evidence that she heard from God during the waiting. While Simeon watched in the waiting, Anna worshiped in the waiting. Both are powerful examples of how God works in and through us, even when it feels like He is taking longer than we think He should.

There have been multiple seasons of my life when I was forced to wait on God. I wish I could say that I am a "good" waiter. I am not. I recall one season specifically when I was anxiously stewing about a situation I had no control over. I clearly remember the moment things changed in my heart. My circumstances didn't change, but the posture of my heart did.

I was on staff at a church at the time, and the church decided to host an all-night worship event from 7:00 p.m. to 7:00 a.m. Different worship bands from various churches came to do a worship set for about an hour at a time, all night long. At some point in the night, I fell asleep worshiping on a bean bag chair that had been moved in from the youth room. I don't remember what songs were being sung or who else was there. What I do remember was spending hours in worship, falling asleep worshiping and waking up worshiping.

Do you know what I *didn't* do that night? I didn't spend all night anxiously worrying about my situation. Instead, I worshiped my way into peace and slept better than I had in years. It was the worship that changed things for me. Since then, when I am tempted to worry and get myself worked up, instead I worship. That lesson has stuck with me because there are always opportunities to wait this side of heaven. But now I have a new strategy that helps me understand *why* Anna stayed at the temple day and night. Inviting God into the pain and anxiety of waiting is the way we get through those seasons. Worship may not change our circumstances, but it changes our hearts. It takes our eyes off the thing we are waiting for and places them on God. How do we handle the seasons that seem longer than we can bear?

We worship in the waiting.

NINETEEN

Prayer and Fasting

Anna worshiped in the waiting, but that's not all she did. In addition to worshiping day and night, she engaged in two other spiritual practices that had an enormous impact on her relationship with God. Let's revisit her story in the book of Luke:

> There was also a prophet, Anna, the daughter of Penuel, of the tribe of Asher. She was very old; she had lived with her husband seven years after her marriage, and then was a widow until she was eighty-four. She never left the temple but worshiped night and day, fasting and praying. Coming up to them at that very moment, she gave thanks to God and spoke about the child to all who were looking forward to the redemption of Jerusalem. (2:36–38)

Did you see it? Anna committed herself to fasting and praying. Before you roll your eyes and skip forward to the next section, I want to draw your attention to something else. Do you see what verse 38 says? It says that she came up to them (Jesus, Mary, and Joseph) at "that very moment."

Anna's timing was not a coincidence. It was evidence that she had been preparing herself through fasting and prayer. We already know that prayer is essentially having a conversation with God. But would you say that fasting is just as high a priority? If you had asked me this years ago, I would have said no. Fasting is really hard to do and can feel overwhelming.

Until you do it.

It's not that the physical act of fasting gets easier. We are human, and it is part of our biology to get hungry. But once you start seeing the results of fasting, you quickly realize that the benefits and the outcome of the fast far outweigh its temporary discomfort. In fact, you can use the hunger pangs as reminders to pray. In all honesty, I learned that the hard way. Early on in my fasting days, those hunger pangs prompted me to pray for the fast to be over quickly, for the Lord to take my mind off food, or for the hunger itself to dull. While those prayers were selfish, they did establish a pattern that drove me back to the Lord over and over. Eventually, my prayers started including other people. Before long, the hunger pangs were the physical clues I needed to remind me of why I was fasting in the first place: to pray.

Once I started to realize that the spiritual practice of fasting was actually leading me closer to the Lord, especially when fasting was combined with prayer, I understood how important fasting is when it comes to posturing our hearts before the Lord. I have seen breakthrough after breakthrough during my weeks of fasting. So much so that it is a regular part of my "spiritual rule," or the rhythms in my year that help me to hear from God.

There have been times in my life when the church I attended held a fast, and I half-heartedly participated. I may have said I was skipping breakfast (which I always do) and giving up sugar. But overall, I would end up forgetting all about the fast by the end of the week, only to feel shame once I went back to church on Sunday.

That's not what I am talking about. What I *am* talking about are those times in my life when I felt God call me to Himself. Times when I knew I needed more of Him. When I needed an answer to a specific prayer. When I needed to rekindle my relationship with Him, which had started to feel dry. Sometimes I was responding in obedience to the prompting of the Holy Spirit. Inevitably, though, during those times of self-denial I truly started to learn how to hear God's voice more clearly. Hunger pangs became reminders to pray. Lunchtime became the time in my day that was freed up to worship.

Can I share something with you? I really hope that by this point you say yes.

As I was writing this section on Anna, I remembered that I had done a week on my podcast talking about the spiritual discipline of fasting.[1] If you are not familiar with spiritual disciplines, they are different skills we can use to build our spiritual muscles to help us grow in our spiritual lives. They are similar to doing reps at a gym that helps us build muscle so we are physically strong.

I dug out the transcript to that podcast episode and started to read through it. I was reading my own words about fasting and what the Lord was teaching me during that specific fast. Do you know what word the Lord gave me during that time?

Faithful remnant.

I don't think it's a coincidence that I was literally in the middle of writing about Anna, who was part of the faithful remnant of Israel. That's a sacred echo. Do you know what a sacred echo is? It's a moment when we sense that God is repeating Himself to make sure we hear Him. I don't know about you, but sometimes I can be a hardhead. I need God to repeat things to me a couple times before I recognize that it's Him. He is so faithful and kind that He often does just that.

Fasting, prayer, and worship. These are the ways I hear from God. These are the ways Anna heard from God. And these are the ways *you* can hear from God.

At the time of that podcast, I didn't fully grasp what God was saying to me in the moment. But I do now. God was setting the stage, speaking a word into my heart that I wouldn't fully understand until years later. *Years* later, while I was writing a book about a woman who was a faithful remnant.

God is so good.

Nothing in Anna's life was an accident or coincidence. And truth be told, as much as we may admire Anna, she was not that different from you and me. While you may not be in the same situation she was, I know that the fact that you are reading this book means you are at least curious about hearing God's voice more clearly. I also know that there will be moments of pain and brokenness in your life—they're part of the human experience. Anna's examples of fasting and prayer are tools that God can use in your life.

If only you let Him.

TWENTY

Running Your Mouth

A faithful remnant.

Worshiping in the waiting.

Dedicated to prayer and fasting.

The only woman in the New Testament to be called a prophet.

These are all amazing things about Anna, but none of them is the most significant. So what is?

Anna was the first person to bear witness to Jesus. Simeon was there, that is true, but Simeon kept the fulfillment of the promise in his life a secret. But Anna? Well, she did what women do best: She ran her mouth.

> She gave thanks to God and spoke about the child to all who were looking forward to the redemption of Jerusalem. (Luke 2:38)

In this case, running her mouth wasn't a bad thing. Instead, it was the very first time anyone declared that Jesus was the Messiah out loud. Think about what would have happened if she had given up on the waiting. What if she had allowed her grief, her poverty, or her situation in life to keep her from drawing close to God? She would have missed the greatest moment of her life, the moment she had so long been waiting for. Instead, we see a woman who remained faithful to God until the very end. In a time when many had turned their backs on the idea of a Messiah, Anna remained faithful. When so many in the tribe of Asher had turned their backs on God, Anna's family remained faithful. In a time when the testimony of women, especially widowed women, was not valued or recognized in a court of law, Anna remained faithful. Her words became a testimony of Jesus. For the very first time.

There were many obstacles Anna could have blamed if she had decided to let go of her relationship with God. I think we do that sometimes in our own lives.

Life gets hard.

Grief knocks us off our feet.

A lack of finances wipes us out.

People in our lives tell us to shut our mouths.

The weight of brokenness feels too heavy.

The list could go on and on. For many of us, the enemy has used our difficulties to keep us from fulfilling God's plan for us.

But Anna? She was present when the baby Jesus arrived on the scene because she believed God's Word until the very end. And in all likelihood, that day probably started like any other. She was doing what she did every day. She was listening for the voice of God as she worshiped, fasted, and prayed.

She stayed present in the promise and lived with the expectation of hearing His voice. She kept doing, faithfully, what God called her to do.

My husband says I talk to breathe, and he's not wrong. I even talk in my sleep. Thankfully, the Lord has redeemed that part of my life in ways that now bless other people.

I remember being at a MOPS meeting one time when they were talking about the body of Christ. I proudly declared that I was pretty sure I was His mouth. While that got a few laughs at the time, it's not that far from the truth. Now I teach, write, speak, and podcast about Jesus all day, every day. As I surrendered my heart (and my mouth) to Him, He allowed me to be used in a way that makes sense for the way He created me. It took a lot of lessons learned on how to be obedient to God before I got here, but I am so glad that He remains faithful. It took not just seasons but entire years of honoring God with my words privately before any of those words ever became public.

How did that transition happen? I wonder if you can guess.

Through worship. God transformed my heart in worship. God revealed His heart in worship. Worship is the thing that takes our focus off ourselves and puts it back on Him. In worship we give God attention, glory, even time. It's worship that changes our hearts. It's worship that provides space for us to have an authentic interaction with Jesus.

Worship helps us, just like Anna and so many others, to see Jesus and to bear witness to His presence in our lives.

When was the last time you intentionally spent a moment in a posture of worship? And I don't mean a Sunday morning service. I mean time that you specifically set aside to just worship Jesus.

Has it been a while?

Friend, go run your mouth for Jesus. In a good way. Go ahead, I'll wait.

TWENTY-ONE

How to Be Like Anna

After all this talk about "running your mouth for Jesus," do you still feel any objection in your spirit? Are there obstacles that pop into your mind when you think about what it would look like to actually live your life like that?

We may compare our own lives to Anna's. She *lived* at the temple. She had no one to take care of. She didn't have a house she had to clean or a nine-to-five job she had to commute to. She didn't have the limitations we have today or even the objections from those around us.

Reflecting on Anna's life can make it easy to justify why we struggle to prioritize prayer, fasting, and worship. But let me clue you in on something: Anna's life was anything but simple. See, even though this story where we meet her takes place "at the temple," she was not actually allowed to enter it.

The events we have been studying in these last few chapters —involving Simeon, Anna, Jesus, and His family—didn't happen inside the temple. They actually happened outside it, in the women's court. How do we know this? Well, a couple of reasons.

First, Mary was present. Second, Anna was present. Women were allowed in only the outer court that was designated for women.

When Scripture refers to the temple, it can actually mean a few different things, depending on the time of history we are talking about. The temple was originally built by Solomon, but that temple was destroyed. Then Zerubbabel built the second temple after the people returned from exile in Babylon. But that temple was also pretty much destroyed. Then King Herod rebuilt the second temple, and this is the temple where Anna's story takes place (see fig. 21.1). Herod's elaborate rebuild included an outer court for the Gentiles, which was the only place non-Jews could go. This is where Jesus flipped over the tables of the money changers. The inner court contained the women's court and the court of Israel. Men and women could both be in the women's court, but only Jewish men could be in the court of Israel. Then there was the court of priests, and as you can imagine, only the priests could enter. That is where they carried out their priestly duties. Finally, there was the Holy of Holies. Only the high priest could enter it.

Anna never made it past the women's court. She never stepped foot inside the actual temple. But she did not allow the limitations placed on her to keep her from doing what God called her to do. She never stopped serving at the temple, worshiping, or praying. She worshiped like it was her job—in a place that she wasn't even welcome to enter fully.

Figure 21.1 **Temple Layout**

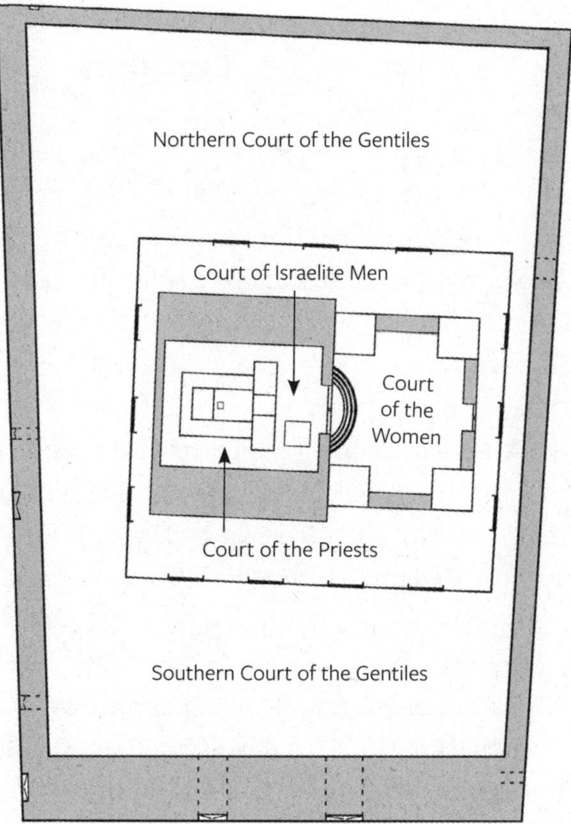

I wonder if that speaks to you the way it speaks to me.

There have been times in my life when I felt like I didn't get access the way my male counterparts did. Or perhaps the cultural restrictions made me feel insecure or like I didn't belong.

Anna wasn't immune to those things; she just didn't let them stop her. They didn't limit her devotion or dedication. The result?

It wasn't the high priest inside the Holy of Holies who was the first person to bear witness to Jesus.

It wasn't even Simeon, a devout Jewish man.

It was Anna.

The first person to declare Jesus as the Christ was a woman.

There were actually very few people who recognized Jesus when He came. Some Gentile wise men recognized Him. Some shepherds in a field recognized Him. Mary and Joseph, of course, recognized Him. And Simeon and Anna recognized Him. That was it.

Why do you think that is?

Besides the fact that many people had given up on the idea of a Messiah coming to save the people of Israel, there are other reasons people may have missed Him.

There have been times in my own life when I almost missed Jesus because He didn't show up in the way I expected Him to. Sometimes I wasn't even looking for Him to show up. I was perfectly content, living my life in my own way, and I wasn't even paying attention to what God was doing. Times when I was even serving in "ministry" but operating in my own strength, completely leaving the Holy Spirit behind at the church. I am not proud of those moments, but I share them to show that we can all have them. We can all be guilty of forgetting to look for Jesus, even if we, in theory, are expecting Him. So often we decide what to do and ask God to bless it. We get the idea from God, but then we shut the door and forget to take Him along on the very job He asked us to do. This doesn't make sense, but we all do it. Instead, let's ask God what *His* agenda is and how we can come alongside Him and help Him.

Everything will change when we start approaching our lives that way, when we seek God's agenda over our agenda.

Simeon and Anna were not serving God the way we often do. Simeon and Anna were serving God with expectation. Simeon was watching in the waiting. Anna was worshiping in the waiting. Their hearts were prepared to see Jesus, whenever, wherever, and however He came. Sometimes Jesus shows up in our lives in a way that is unexpected. Don't miss Jesus showing up in your life because you aren't expecting Him.

Don't miss Jesus showing up in your life because you aren't expecting Him.

God values the voices of women, even if the world around us doesn't. Don't allow the restrictions of the world, or even the church, to keep you from your dedication to the Lord. Worship like it's your job, and then hearing God's voice will be the side effect.

Our deepest longing—to see Jesus—is satisfied when we live in a place of worship.

How do we see Jesus? When we

worship
fast
pray
serve
worship some more

Like that of Anna, let our stories start and end with worship.

QUESTIONS TO PONDER

- Have you experienced any sacred echoes in your spiritual journey? How did they impact your faith or your confidence in what it is like to experience and understand that God is speaking to you?
- Anna is described as a "faithful remnant" of Israel. How does her faithfulness inspire you to remain committed to God, even in challenging circumstances?
- Do you currently have a promise from God you are waiting on? How does it feel to be in a season of waiting? Are there moments when you feel like giving up?
- Anna worshiped night and day despite her difficult circumstances. How can you incorporate worship into your daily life, especially during challenging seasons?
- Anna's encounter with Jesus was perfectly timed. How have you seen God's timing play out in your own life? What role do you think fasting and prayer might have in aligning your timing with God's will?

Reflect on the fact that the first person to declare Jesus as the Christ was a woman. Consider how this impacts your understanding of how God values women's voices, especially in a spiritual context. Pray about how this might encourage you to use your voice in your own faith journey.

KNOWING GOD'S VOICE IN REAL LIFE

The Necklace

I was recently invited to speak to a local group about missions at a banquet. Glad for the invitation, as well as a meal with some kind people, I started to think through what I was going to wear. Realizing that I didn't have any accessories to go with the outfit I wanted to wear, I decided to pick up a couple new pieces of jewelry. A pair of earrings, a new bracelet, a necklace. Just enough for me to feel polished and pretty.

The evening for the dinner came, and it felt special to put on the new jewelry for the first time. We had a sweet time of fellowship in which I was able to share God's heart for the nations as well as the opportunities He was giving me over the next couple months. A mom and her two young daughters were sitting right up front, and they invited me to sit with them for dinner after I finished speaking. The youngest daughter sat next to me and was fascinated with my new necklace. Her little fingers kept rubbing the pearls. One of the times she did that, the Holy Spirit gently told me to give the necklace to her.

I wish I could say I had a cheerful heart in that moment, but the truth is I argued with God. It was brand-new! And it was the first time I had ever worn it! And it matched my earrings and bracelet!

Give it to her.

Feeling almost scolded, I took off the necklace and placed it around the neck of this sweet little girl. Her beaming smile erased any leftover selfish feelings I had, as I saw how much it blessed her. Later I learned that it was actually the little girl's birthday. The meal we were sharing was the only way the family could afford to eat out, because someone in the group had invited them and had already paid for their food. Suddenly, it made sense why the Lord told me to give her the necklace.

The end of the evening came, and as we were saying our goodbyes, the little girl handed me my necklace. She thanked me for letting her borrow it because wearing it during her birthday dinner had made her feel so beautiful and special. This time there was no hesitation in my heart as I put the necklace back on her. "Keep it," I whispered. "Jesus wants you to have it." Her smile alone was payment enough, and I could feel how much it blessed her. The girl's mother, with tears welling up, thanked me with a hug and left. They were visiting from out of town, so I assumed I would never see them again.

A few months later, I was cleaning up the nursery after church and walked into the lobby to grab a cup of coffee. As I did, I was surprised to see the young mother standing there. I quickly gave her a hug, and she sheepishly looked down. I looked down as well and saw a worn, white envelope in her hand. She pushed the envelope into my hands and then ran out the front door. Shocked by what had just happened, I walked into a private area and opened the envelope. Inside I found two hundred dollars and a note that simply said, "This is for you."

I knew this young mother didn't have two hundred dollars to spare. I knew this money cost her something. The necklace I had given her daughter cost nowhere near two hundred dollars. Yet I also knew that the Lord saw her sacrifice, her obedience to Him. Even if I never see her again, I know that He sees her.

I don't think God told me to give that twenty-dollar necklace away just so I could later get two hundred dollars. I think God told me to give that necklace away because of how much it would bless that sweet girl. I think God told me to give that necklace away to test my obedience. I think God told me to give that necklace away so I could experience His heart for that little girl in a way that was tangible and real. And I also think God was working in the heart of that young mother. Her obedience was a blessing to me in a very similar way that my obedience was a blessing to her.

As we are obedient to God's voice, it becomes more clear.

PART 5

ENCOURAGEMENT FOR TODAY'S PROPHETS

TWENTY-TWO

Getting It Wrong

Scripture is full of some amazing examples of women whom God placed in leadership within their circles of influence. He gave them wonderful gifts to be used for His glory as they spoke God's word to God's people. But I would be doing you a disservice if I didn't also point out that sometimes there were women who got it wrong. There are a variety of reasons why this happened in Scripture, just like there are a variety of reasons why this happens today. Sometimes it was a symptom of their heart and the fact that they were intentionally trying to manipulate others for control or other nefarious reasons. We see this in a woman named Noadiah in the Old Testament book of Nehemiah. We have only one line about her:

> Remember also the prophet Noadiah and how she and the rest of the prophets have been trying to intimidate me. (6:14)

Even if you don't know the entire backstory, it's clear that Noadiah was using a false word from God to intimidate God's people. In this case, she was intentionally trying to cause division among the Jews. She had been bribed to distract Nehemiah from rebuilding the wall around the city.

The enemy will often pervert and twist things in the name of God in order to offer a counterfeit version of God's plan. It's kind of his MO. He has been doing it since the dawn of time. This is why I say over and over that God's voice will never contradict God's Word. God's Word is the primary way we hear His voice. If someone says something that is contrary to what God has already said in His Word, then it's not God's voice. We need to be diligent about testing any prophetic words that come from those we interact with.

Sometimes, though, it's not intentional when someone "gets it wrong." Sometimes it's spiritual immaturity, and people are too new in their faith to know better. Or perhaps someone has fallen under faulty teaching that has led them down a faulty path. Even though those people may have good intentions, a false word can be damaging. We need to hold this gift carefully, making 100 percent sure we are in line with God's heart before we share what we say are His words. Otherwise, we can do so much damage.

One of the most common barriers to the idea of prophecy within the body of Christ is the exposure many of us have had to false prophecies. There is never a shortage of discredited TV preachers who claim to know when the world will end, when Jesus will come back, or that you will be healed if you send them ninety-nine dollars. These tactics can be so damaging, and I truly believe they are used by the enemy to keep people from experiencing God through prophecy.

I clearly remember the day someone declared a false prophecy over me. I was getting ready to take the stage to preach at a church. I was in the hallway, praying, getting ready for the host to introduce me. Just moments before having to focus on the message the Lord had given me for this particular audience, a woman came up to me to tell me that she had a word for me. In the moment, I didn't really have a reason to question or doubt, thinking that because I was in a church, I was in a safe place. The woman went on to tell me that my child was in danger of a sexual assault. As you can imagine, as a mom of three young girls, I started to panic a bit. Thinking through where my girls were at that moment, I prayed for them as I took the stage. There wasn't even time to respond to this woman, only to pray.

Let me tell you that, first of all, I am so thankful for the Holy Spirit. One of His roles is the comforter. In His wisdom, He led me to reject and rebuke that word in my spirit. Almost immediately, I was flooded with the kind of peace that can come only from God. A kind of peace that calmed my anxious mama's heart and allowed me to minister to the people of God.

My children were fine. I was fine. Everything was fine. Yet the enemy had crept in, using the woman's words to impact my heart and mind, even if only briefly. But this incident helped me to understand how important it is for both the person giving a prophetic word and the person receiving a word to make sure that the word truly is from God.

How do we do that? Well, think about what we talked about earlier in this book. What does the New Testament say about prophecy? It is used to exhort, edify, and console

(1 Cor. 14:3–4). Remember, only 8 percent of the Old Testament prophecies were foretelling. The other 92 percent were reminding people what God had already said. The word this woman shared did not encourage, edify, or console me. Instead, it produced fear and anxiety in me right before I was about to share God's Word.

Fear and anxiety are not from God. Period. If that word had been from God, I don't think He would have delivered it right before I was about to share the gospel with a thousand people. If that word had been from God, it would have been a benefit to me, not a detriment. If that word had been from God, it likely would have confirmed something I was already seeking Him about.

That word was not from God.

So, what do we do when we receive a word from the Lord? Here are some important points that I think we need to keep in mind when it comes to giving and receiving a word from God.

1. Be careful whom you allow to speak into your life. Sometimes you will hear this called "testing the spirit." I should have prayed, even if quickly, before I allowed that woman to share a word. In all honesty, I didn't think to. Again, I thought I was safe because I was in a church. Let me tell you right now that sometimes the devil finds his way into the four walls of a church. In fact, it's where he does some of his best work. Just because someone calls themselves a Christian or shows up at church doesn't mean they are safe and someone you should allow to speak into your life. Always, always, always pray for God to show you if someone is safe or not.

2. God's voice will never contradict God's Word.

I know I've said this before. A lot. But I really, really mean it. If someone claims to have heard God's voice but what they say conflicts with God's Word, then it wasn't God's voice. I am not necessarily saying this woman had evil intentions. Perhaps she had some anxiety or trauma in her own life that she was projecting onto me. I don't really know the reason she said what she did, but it's clear she had heard some faulty teaching on how prophecy works. Even if, and that is a *big* even if, God showed me a pressing word of caution for someone, I would never go up to them right before they were going to share the gospel message in front of a crowd. I would wait until I had time to sit with them, pray with them, come up with a strategy. I would at least wait until after they were done teaching onstage. A word from God will comfort us, not put us in a tailspin. Measure any word that comes to you through the lens of God's Word.

3. A word from God will not add to or take away from Scripture.

I know this sounds similar to my last point, but I want to elaborate on it a little bit. Sometimes someone will share a word that they say is a "new" revelation from God or is different from what God's Word actually says. A prophetic word that adds to Scripture or changes Scripture is a false prophecy. Period. So for those in the back of the room, let me say it again: God's voice will never contradict God's Word.

4. Ask God if it's true.

This may go without saying, but ask God if the word resonates with your spirit. If you are a believer and have put your faith in Jesus, then you have a relationship with Him. Just ask Him. It may be that the word wasn't for you but for the person sitting next to you. Or perhaps it's for future you. Prophecy is one of those gifts we learn more about the more we practice it and are obedient. But ultimately, we are human; we are not God. Even if we are regularly hearing from God, we aren't perfect, and this side of heaven, we may make mistakes. The beauty is that we each have a unique relationship with God that gives us access to Him 24/7. If you are unsure about something, just ask Him.

5. Hold the gift responsibly.

If you sense that God is giving you knowledge and wisdom to share with someone else, realize what an amazing responsibility that is. Sometimes our own emotions or our own filter can get in the way of what the Lord is trying to say. The key to growing in this gift is abiding in Christ. Listening to what He says starts with knowing and being obedient to His Word. If you have the gift of prophecy, don't take it for granted. Don't abuse the trust God has given you. This is a line that gets crossed in the church and leads to so much damage. Damage that can have eternal consequences. Realize the immense responsibility God has given you with this gift.

6. Make sure God is telling you to share.

Sometimes God will give you something to share with others, and sometimes God will give you something that is just for you. Even if what He gives you is for other people, hold on to it until God gives you the go-ahead. How will you know? Trust me, you'll know. Prayerfully ask God to show you. Who?

When? How? All of those are just as important as the message itself. Obedience is not always about speaking out what God has said. Sometimes it's about holding it.

7. Edify/exhort/console.

I cannot emphasize this enough. The gift of prophecy should always encourage, comfort, and lift others up. It should not be used to control someone or a situation or to manipulate. Always look through this lens. A word from God will bless someone. Even if it is a word of conviction from the Holy Spirit, that word will still be a blessing because it will point someone back to Christ.

TWENTY-THREE

Getting It Right

Now that we have addressed "getting it wrong," I have some additional thoughts about "getting it right."

There are many more examples in Scripture about women who heard clearly from the Lord and acted on those words. Sometimes they shared those words from the Lord, and sometimes they just allowed those words to encourage and equip them to do the things God called them to do. I encourage you to keep this in mind the next time you read about various women in the Bible. Here are a few to get you started:

Sarah (see Gen. 11–12, 15–18, 21, 23)

Rebekah (see Gen. 24–25, 27)

Hannah (see 1 Sam. 1–2)

Esther (see Esth. 1–10)

The daughters of the people who prophesy in Ezekiel (see Ezek. 13)

The daughters of Heman, who served King David (see 1 Chron. 25)

Abigail (see 1 Sam. 25)

Isaiah's wife (see Isa. 8)

Philip's daughters (see Acts 21)

Elizabeth (see Luke 1)

Mary, mother of Jesus (see Luke 1–2; John 2, 19; Acts 1)

The daughters Joel says will prophesy (see Joel 2; Acts 2)

I want to spend a minute talking about that last suggestion, because it includes you and me. If you are unfamiliar, this is what the prophet Joel had to say in Joel 2:28–29:

> And afterward,
> I will pour out my Spirit on all people.
> Your sons and daughters will prophesy,
> your old men will dream dreams,
> your young men will see visions.
> Even on my servants, both men and women,
> I will pour out my Spirit in those days.

Joel was looking forward to the time when the Holy Spirit would be poured out on the earth. Do you want to know some *really* good news? That's already happened. God fulfilled Joel's prophecy with an outpouring of the Holy Spirit at Pentecost. You can read about it in Acts 2. We see later in the New Testament that the apostle Paul encourages all believers to seek this spiritual gift to edify the church:

> Follow the way of love and eagerly desire gifts of the Spirit, especially prophecy. (1 Cor. 14:1)

Peter talks about this as well in the New Testament, echoing what the prophet Joel said in the Old Testament:

> Even on my servants, both men and women,
> I will pour out my Spirit in those days,
> and they will prophesy. (Acts 2:18)

Friends, do you see what I am getting at? Women being included in this spiritual gift, speaking God's word to God's people, is part of God's plan.

And it always has been.

TWENTY-FOUR

God Is Always the Hero

As we finish up our time together, it is my prayer that the end of this book is not the end of your desire to learn about and operate within the spiritual gift of hearing from God. Instead, I hope it's the beginning. As you learn more about how God speaks to believers but specifically to *you*, things will become clearer. I know I have said this several times throughout this book, but you *must* spend time with God in order to learn what His voice sounds like. When I talk about spending time with God, I mean things like reading and studying His Word. Spending dedicated time in worship outside of a Sunday morning. Fasting with the intention of denying yourself so you can focus on God. Then be obedient when you *do* hear His voice. Be a good steward of the gifts He has already given you. Lay aside pride for humility. Above all, know God and make Him known.

That being said, I want you to give yourself grace in this area. There is always a learning curve when we first start practicing any of the spiritual gifts. There will be times you mess up, get it wrong, or are too fearful to be obedient. I get it. I've been there. However, I have a few pointers based on my own missteps and confirmations.

First, a humble heart that seeks to be obedient to the Lord is a heart that is primed to hear His voice. Everything circles back to making sure you are remaining obedient to God's Word and God's voice.

Second, always ask permission before sharing. I mean this in two ways. First, ask God if you can or *should* share what He is showing you. If He doesn't give the go-ahead, then hold His word in your heart. Maybe He will reveal when and if you are to share, and maybe He won't. Either way, obedience is key. Second, assuming the Holy Spirit has given you the go-ahead, ask permission from the person before you share with them. We never know where people are at spiritually, or even emotionally. Most will want you to share, but some will not be ready to receive. If that is the case, don't take offense. Instead, pray for them. Be sensitive to their reaction. Sometimes, as I shared earlier, I will write down an "undelivered" message from the Lord. This helps to clear out head space and heart space so that I can pray for that person without feeling so burdened to share with them. Perhaps the time to share will come, or perhaps the message will give you insight on how to pray for them. Either way, prayerfully seek the Lord in how to handle the situation. Obedience is always more important than outcome.

Third, often the gift of discernment goes hand in hand with the gift of hearing God's voice. Sometimes the Holy Spirit will disrupt your peace when someone is speaking a false word. In those moments, it is not just appropriate to speak up but part of being a truth teller. If you are in a public setting like a church and you know that someone is manipulating God's Word, you may need to get up and walk out. It may not be appropriate to immediately say something. However, following up the "walkout" with a one-on-one conversation is necessary.

We live in an age when many megachurch pastors have fallen from grace because of their behavior. These are typically men at large churches with many people on their staff. I have to wonder how many times women remained silent when they should have been speaking out. There is a way to speak the truth in love, but these kinds of situations do not happen in a vacuum. There are people who are remaining silent that God has called to speak up. It is my prayer that you will have a better understanding now of how God wants you to use your voice and the impact it can make.

Finally, after studying the powerful accounts of these women in the Bible, we may look at them as heroes. They have some pretty incredible stories about how God used them.

Miriam celebrated God's deliverance and spoke to Israel on God's behalf during one of the most difficult seasons of Israel's history. Her heart for worship taught the women of Israel about being prepared to worship, no matter what the circumstances.

Miriam is not the hero.

Deborah was not only a judge and leader in Israel but also a prophetess who rode into battle and helped bring a victory that gave God's people peace for the next forty years. She was a victorious warrior.

Deborah is not the hero.

Huldah was called upon by the king of Israel to authenticate the Book of the Law. She called out God's people for their sin and spoke forgiveness over the king.

Huldah is not the hero.

Anna was the first person to bear witness to Jesus and a faithful servant of God until the very end of her life.

Anna is not the hero.

When God uses you to speak His word to His people, you are not the hero.

God is always the hero.

Scripture reveals to us the God of the Bible . . . His character, His nature. Those things do not change. The way He works through individual lives sometimes changes, but He does not change. Anytime God uses anyone, any good outcome is only because He is the one authoring it.

We must remember that when God uses us, God is always the hero.

QUESTIONS TO PONDER

- Consider the fear and anxiety produced by a false prophecy. How can you differentiate between a word that is truly from God and one that causes unnecessary fear and anxiety? What role does peace play in discerning God's voice?
- God's voice will never contradict God's Word. Have you encountered situations in which someone claimed to have a word from God that conflicted with Scripture? Have you ever been that person? Spend some time reflecting on how you can handle that situation differently next time.
- Think about the responsibility that comes with the gift of prophecy. If you believe God is giving you a word to share with someone, how do you ensure that you handle that responsibility with care? What steps can you take to confirm that the word is truly from God and meant to be shared?
- Reflect on the concept of holding on to a word until God gives you the go-ahead to share it. Have you ever felt prompted to wait before sharing something God revealed to you? How did that experience shape your understanding of obedience and timing in sharing God's messages?
- The purpose of prophecy is to edify, exhort, and console. How does this understanding of prophecy

influence how you receive and give prophetic words? What practices can you adopt to ensure that any word you share aligns with this purpose?

Reflect on the truth that despite their amazing stories, the women in the Bible are not the heroes. God is. Allow this to shift the way you view your own role in God's work. Make sure He remains the hero in your own life.

Acknowledgments

I would like to thank my agent, Whitney Gossett of New Bridge, for believing in me from the very beginning. Without you championing me, this book would not be what it is. I so appreciate you.

I would also like to thank my friends at Compassion International for their support and for providing a way for me to continually live on mission. Go check out Compassion.com/HearingJesus.

For my Oskavon family, I am so thankful for the way God has used you as part of my process as we learn together what it means to hear God's voice.

For my sisters in Christ, who build me up when I am discouraged, who pray me through when I am weary, and who celebrate with me in moments that bear witness to the goodness of God, I love you.

And to my family, thank you for loving me, for allowing me to verbally process at the dinner table, and for asking the questions that make my brain hurt. I love you all to the end of eternity.

And most of all, thank you to Jesus. It brings me to tears to think of the amazing privilege it is to be able to speak into this place. I am so thankful for Your tender voice, which speaks love to places that I keep sealed off from everyone else.

Notes

CHAPTER 2 SHADOWS OF FAITH

1. Gordon Fee, *How to Read the Bible for All Its Worth* (Zondervan, 2014), 182.

CHAPTER 4 LEPROSY OF THE HEART

1. *Easton's Bible Dictionary*, under "leprosy," Bible Gateway, accessed January 15, 2025, https://www.biblegateway.com/resources/eastons-bible-dictionary/leprosy; Tamar Fox, "Tzaraat—A Biblical Affliction," My Jewish Learning, accessed January 15, 2025, https://www.myjewishlearning.com/article/tzaraat-a-biblical-affliction/; Robert S. Kawashima, "Leprosy (Word Study)," Bible Odyssey, accessed January 15, 2025, https://behappyhuman.bibleodyssey.org/articles/leprosy-word-study.

2. Shlomo Yaffe, "Healing Hubris," Chabad.org, accessed February 10, 2025, https://www.chabad.org/parshah/article_cdo/aid/663582/jewish/Healing-Hubris.htm; Rachel Adler, "A Disease That Walls Get? Decoding Tzaraat and Facing Our Fears," ReformJudaism.org, accessed February 10, 2025, https://reformjudaism.org/learning/torah-study/torah-commentary/disease-walls-get-decoding-tzaraat-and-facing-our-fears.

CHAPTER 5 HOW TO BE LIKE MIRIAM

1. Jonathan Stokl and Corrine L. Carvalho, eds., *Prophets Male and Female: Gender and Prophecy in the Hebrew Bible, the Eastern Mediterranean, and the Ancient Near East* (Society of Biblical Literature, 2013), 157–62.

CHAPTER 6 A COUNTERCULTURAL IDENTITY

1. *Abarim Publications Biblical Dictionary*, under "Deborah," accessed February 5, 2025, https://www.abarim-publications.com/Meaning/Deborah.html?utm_source.

2. Margaret Mowczko, "What's in a Name? Deborah, Woman of Lappidoth," *Marg Mowczko* (blog), November 28, 2015, https://margmowczko.com/deborah-woman-of-lappidoth/.

3. Chaim Bentorah, "Hebrew Word Study—Deborah," Chaim Bentorah: Biblical Hebrew Studies, November 24, 2019, https://www.chaimbentorah.com/2019/11/hebrew-word-study-deborah/.
4. Mowczko, "What's in a Name?"

CHAPTER 7 A WOMAN OF INFLUENCE

1. Stephen J. Bramer, "Appendix 1: Understanding the Prophets," Bible.org, accessed October 28, 2024, https://bible.org/seriespage/appendix-1-understanding-prophets?utm_source.

CHAPTER 12 DON'T STAY SILENT

1. "10 Facts about America's Churchless," Barna Group, December 10, 2014, https://www.barna.com/research/10-facts-about-americas-churchless.

CHAPTER 16 HOW TO BE LIKE HULDAH

1. Spiros Zodhiates, ed., *The Hebrew-Greek Key Word Study Bible* (AMG Publishers, 1990), 1750.
2. Zodhiates, *Hebrew-Greek Key Word Study Bible*, 1780.
3. Zodhiates, *Hebrew-Greek Key Word Study Bible*, 1782.
4. Zodhiates, *Hebrew-Greek Key Word Study Bible*, 1840.

CHAPTER 17 WATCHING IN THE WAITING

1. Zodhiates, *Hebrew-Greek Key Word Study Bible*, 1720, 1765, 1815, 1780.

CHAPTER 18 WORSHIP IN THE WAITING

1. *Easton's Bible Dictionary*, under "Anna," Bible Study Tools, accessed February 7, 2025, https://www.biblestudytools.com/dictionary/anna/?utm_source.

CHAPTER 19 PRAYER AND FASTING

1. *Hearing Jesus* (podcast), episode 591, "Fasting for Beginners—Hearing God's Voice Through Fasting, Devotional," June 26, 2024, https://podcasts.apple.com/ao/podcast/fasting-for-beginners-hearing-gods-voice-through-fasting/id1615623952?i=1000660302331.

About the Author

RACHAEL GROLL is the host of the popular podcasts *Hearing Jesus* and *Hearing Jesus for Kids*. Rachael "talks to breathe," so she is also a writer, speaker, and pastor. She has a heart for helping others hear God's voice more clearly and know God's Word more fully. Her ministry experience spans two decades, in which she has served in both local churches and ministries around the world addressing global orphan care, anti-trafficking, and food insecurity. Rachael holds an MA in Bible Exposition/Theology from Biola University Talbot School of Theology and a BA in Ministerial Leadership from Southeastern University. When she isn't writing, she spends her time with her husband, Tim, and her three beautiful daughters in rural Pennsylvania. Her goal is to know Him and to make Him known. That's her goal for you too.

CONNECT WITH RACHAEL:

WEB SHEHEARS.ORG

FACEBOOK @SHEHEARS.ORG

INSTAGRAM @RACHAEL.D.GROLL